LOST RAILWAYS
OF
STAFFORDSHIRE

LOST RAILWAYS OF STAFFORDSHIRE

Leslie Oppitz

COUNTRYSIDE BOOKS
NEWBURY, BERKSHIRE

COUNTRYSIDE BOOKS
3 Catherine Road
Newbury, Berkshire

To view our complete range of books,
please visit us at
www.countrysidebooks.co.uk

ISBN 1 85306 992 2
EAN 978 1 85306 992 5

The cover picture shows
the LMS Jubilee class locomotive 4-6-0 *Leander* No 5690
hauling an express train through Tamworth (High Level) station
on the line between Burton-upon-Trent and Birmingham,
and is from an original painting by
Colin Doggett

Maps by Jennie Collins

Produced through MRM Associates Ltd., Reading
Typeset by CJWT Solutions, Newton-le-Willows
Printed by Woolnough Bookbinding Ltd., Irthlingborough

CONTENTS

ACKNOWLEDGEMENTS

Acknowledgements and thanks go to the numerous libraries and record offices throughout Staffordshire and many of the surrounding areas for delving into records, and also to the staff at Oswestry library, who never failed to locate an out-of-print book.

Thanks also to the late J. L. Smith of Lens of Sutton and to Paul Bolger of Stations UK, D. K. Jones, Russell Mulford, John H. Meredith, Mark Smith, the Staffordshire County Museum at Shugborough and Andy Parker of the *Burton Mail* for their help in finding many old photographs.

I am also grateful to the following who generously contributed with information: my son Nigel and daughter-in-law Julie, Ian Rutherford of Foxfield Steam Railway, David Bathurst of Chasewater Railway, D. R. Gibson of the Cheddlestone Railway Centre and Peter Bell of the Amerton Narrow Gauge Railway.

Personal thanks go to my wife Joan for travelling Staffordshire with me and also for her careful checking of the final manuscript.

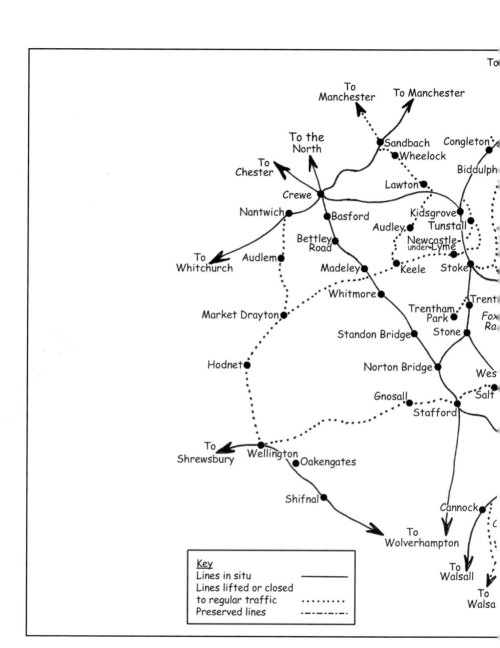

To

To
Manchester   To Manchester

To the
North   Sandbach   Congleton
To   Wheelock
Chester   Biddulph
         Crewe   Lawton
Nantwich   Basford   Kidsgrove
         Bettley   Audley   Tunstall
         Road   Newcastle-
To   under-Lyme
Whitchurch   Audlem   Stoke
         Madeley   Keele
         Whitmore   Trent
                              Trentham   Fox
Market Drayton   Park   Ra
                     Standon Bridge   Stone
Hodnet   Norton Bridge
                                          Wes
                     Gnosall   Salt
To   Stafford
Shrewsbury   Wellington
             Oakengates
                                          Cannock   C
         Shifnal
                         To   To
                    Wolverhampton   Walsall
                                             To
                                          Walsa

Key
Lines in situ   ————
Lines lifted or closed
to regular traffic   ··········
Preserved lines   —·—·—·—

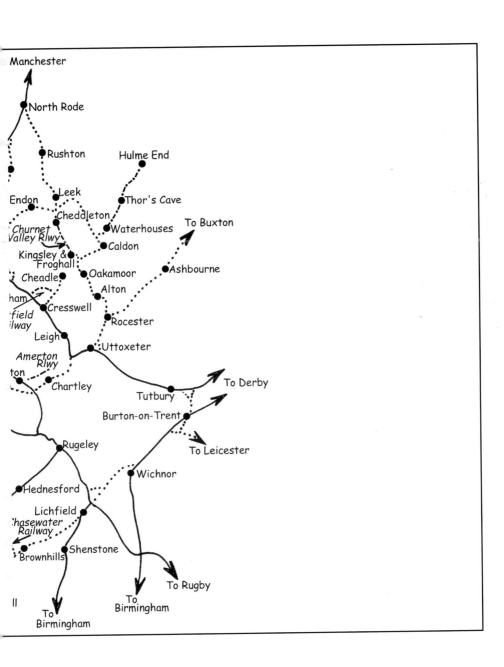

ABBREVIATIONS

BR	British Rail
B&ALR	Burton & Ashby Light Railway
GJR	Grand Junction Railway
GNR	Great Northern Railway
GWR	Great Western Railway
L&BR	London & Birmingham Railway
L&MR	Liverpool & Manchester Railway
L&MVLR	Leek & Manifold Valley Light Railway
LMSR	London, Midland & Scottish Railway
LNER	London & North Eastern Railway
LNWR	London & North Western Railway
MR	Midland Railway
NSR	North Staffordshire Railway
S&BR	Shrewsbury & Birmingham Railway
S&UR	Stafford & Uttoxeter Railway
SSR	South Staffordshire Railway
SUR&CC	Shropshire Union Railways & Canal Company
WCML	West Coast Main Line

Please note:
'Junction' means a railway station
'junction' means where railway lines meet.

Introduction

Austerity locomotive 0-6-0T no 68030, in full steam and hauling coaches, pulled slowly southwards out of Cheddleton station towards Uttoxeter on the Churnet Valley line. This was North Staffordshire Railway (NSR) territory, a company affectionately known as 'Knotty' to its followers because of its use of the Staffordshire knot as its motif. But the train from Cheddleton did not reach Uttoxeter. Instead it travelled just over 10 miles to Kingsley & Froghall and the date was 2nd August 2005. The Victorian country station of Cheddleton closed to passengers over 40 years ago and the venue is currently the headquarters of the North Staffordshire Railway Company (1978) Ltd.

Conventional railways as known today began in the 1820s following George Stephenson's enthusiasm for locomotive engines. With the opening of the Stockton to Darlington Railway in 1825, the first steam train had arrived. Travelling was pretty uncomfortable in those early days. Railway carriages began as stage-coach bodies attached to wagon bases. They were small, cramped and unlit and had no heating or travel facilities. When lighting came it was by oil lamps, subsequently to be replaced by gas lamps. Steam heating and comfortable seating came late in the century and the 1880s saw the introduction of dining cars with equipped kitchens, purpose-built for long-distance travel. It is a sad reflection that the luxuries of Pullman car travel are today almost defunct!

Trains first came to Staffordshire when the Grand Junction Railway opened between Birmingham and Warrington via Crewe on 4th July 1837. The line was of immediate benefit to the Potteries, with coaches offering services by road to and from such places as Whitmore and Madeley. It was a further ten years, December 1847, before the Trent Valley line opened from Rugby to Stafford, another strategically important main line but built to bypass Birmingham and Wolverhampton. The North Staffordshire Railway soon followed, beginning modestly with a stretch from Stoke-on-Trent to Norton Bridge opening in April 1848 to link with the Stafford to Crewe main line. By the end of the year, the NSR had spread in many directions.

From these routes, branch lines developed where steam trains made their way across open stretches of countryside, linking remote villages and towns. In numerous instances passenger traffic remained light throughout, although goods or mineral traffic provided essential services. Some lines suffered an early demise simply because they became uneconomic and, with road transport fast competing, the Beeching cuts of the early 1960s also took their toll.

This book intends to examine the lives of the many 'lost' lines in Staffordshire, as well as their decline and closure. It also includes the preserved lines and societies of today that are dedicated to keeping the past alive. *Lost Railways of Staffordshire* provides the reader with a means to explore numerous closed stations that can be found and the many trackbeds that have survived, some converted to footpaths.

Leslie Oppitz

1
How It All Began: The Grand Junction Railway

Birmingham/Stafford/Crewe

Locomotive 45670 'Howard of Effingham' photographed at Lichfield in August 1956. (D.K. Jones Collection)

Passengers travelling the West Coast Main Line (WCML) today may take for granted a five-hour journey in comparative comfort from London Euston to Glasgow Central. Yet in much earlier times conditions were far from Inter-City standards. Soon after the opening of the Grand Junction Railway (GJR), trains consisted of first and second class coaches, as well as open third class coaches. Only first and second class gave protection from the weather and the latter had no lining or cushions on the seats. Some coaches even had seats on the roof for those who preferred riding outside. Fortunately there were few tunnels – one of 100 yards near Preston Brook must have made for an uncomfortable journey!

The Bill for the Grand Junction Railway was passed in Parliament on 6th May 1833. Three engineers were employed to carry out the work. George Stephenson was in overall control, Joseph Locke took on the northern half and John Rastrick the southern half. Joseph Locke had made a name for himself because of the excellent work he did in the construction of the Liverpool & Manchester Railway. Problems soon developed between the engineers, leading to Rastrick's resignation in September 1833, followed by Stephenson's resignation two years later. The remaining engineer, Joseph Locke, was delighted to take on his new task.

There were construction problems on the outskirts of Birmingham, where a detour was needed requiring a further Act

Rugeley Trent Valley station, photographed in 1957. Apart from being a WCML station, Rugeley is also a junction serving trains to Walsall, Dudley and Kidderminster. (Stations UK)

14

of Parliament. There was another challenge for Locke at Penkridge, between Wolverhampton and Stafford, where a viaduct was necessary. This required seven arches and the foundations had to be buried in concrete to a depth of 70 ft. James Watt, the son of the famous engineer, owned Aston Hall and he was bitterly opposed to a railway passing through his grounds. This needed a quick change of route and the building of extra bridges, viaducts and embankments, which greatly increased Locke's workload. Even so the construction of the line was carried out in record time and it was a great triumph for Locke. The average cost was estimated at less than £20,000 a mile, which was cheap compared with the London & Birmingham Railway at £46,000 a mile.

When completed in 1837, the railway was considered a great success. A reporter from *The Times* travelling on the first train on the morning of the opening day reported, 'The train arrived at Crewe at three minutes to nine o'clock and was received with a hearty welcome by a large concourse of spectators collected together for the occasion.' The *Crewe Guardian* covered the event by reporting, 'There was great rejoicing in the neighbourhood and people came from all over the countryside to witness the strange spectacle. At various points on the line the country folk ran out of their houses to see the strange iron monster go past and wondered what next would be witnessed?'

In the first six months of operation GJR trains carried 232,202 passengers and the company continued to prosper during its life of nine years. In 1838 the GJR introduced a 'convertible bed carriage', which eventually led to today's sleeping car. The comfort of steam heating came first in 1843 although initially applied only to Queen Victoria's Royal Saloon. In 1846 the Grand Junction Railway amalgamated with the London & Birmingham Railway (L&BR) and the Liverpool & Manchester Railway (L&MR) to be known as the London & North Western Railway (LNWR) and to become the country's largest railway company.

The first all-corridor trains to be introduced in the UK came in 1897. Introduced by the LNWR they were used on the 2 pm London–Glasgow service. Following amalgamation in 1923 the

Milford and Brocton station in LNWR days, sited on today's WCML. The station closed in March 1950, with goods facilities closing ten years later. (Stations UK)

LNWR became known as the London, Midland & Scottish Railway (LMS) and four years later in 1927 came the first non-stop services between London and Glasgow. The 10 am train that left London was named 'The Royal Scot'.

Many of the intermediate stations on the Staffordshire section of today's WCML have long since gone. Milford and Brocton closed to passengers in 1950 with Colwich following in 1958. Only one station survives today between Stafford and Crewe. This is Norton Bridge, a short island platform, where trains leave on the former North Staffordshire Railway (NSR) branch to Stone and Stoke. Between Stafford and Norton Bridge, Great Bridgeford station closed in 1949 to passengers. Three years later came the closure of Madeley, Whitmore and Standon Bridge stations although they were once of some importance with horse-drawn coaches offering services to and from the Potteries.

Basford station in Cheshire closed much earlier, in 1875, to make way for track improvements, the area later to become the

LNWR locomotive no 46238 hauls an express train through Standon Bridge in 1949. Standon Bridge station on the WCML closed in February 1952, with goods closure following in 1965. (Stations UK)

extensive Basford Hall Marshalling Yard. This was an LNWR project, which initially employed over 600 men and could handle a daily intake of some 600 wagons. At its peak in the 1930s it was reckoned the yard handled more than 400 trains daily and nearly 50,000 wagons a week. In the 1960s Basford Yard was reconstructed and electrified.

Crewe station is probably one of the most famous worldwide. Before the GJR arrived in 1837 the town had a population of just 184 but when locomotive building began in 1845 the town's future was assured. The LNWR, known as 'The Premier Line', was soon to employ more than 10,000 at Crewe. The station has of course seen many changes. From its modest beginnings, track improvements have been implemented over the years and within this decade a West Coast modernisation programme has been put in hand to upgrade track and signalling to raise maximum speeds to a potential of 125 mph. Earlier modernisation in 1985 at Crewe meant that six signal boxes were closed.

A lone spectator on a wet day watches a passing train at Tamworth High Level station in 1950. Here passengers could change for trains on the WCML. (Stations UK)

Crewe station platform 1 in LNWR days, c1910. Platform 1 was renumbered platform 14 and today it connects only with local sidings. (Stations UK)

Not far from Crewe station can be found the Crewe Arms Hotel, which was originally built in 1837 by Lord Crewe. It was described as 'very fair accommodation and often providing, about one o'clock, a fine hot joint of grass-fed beef of magnificent dimensions'. In September 1848 Queen Victoria and her suite stayed there, having given the inn-keeper no notice of arrival. The Queen was travelling south from Scotland by train and decided to break 'her tedious journey' at Crewe. In 1864 the hotel was leased to the LNWR, which had the building enlarged although retaining its original style architecture, but today is once again in private hands.

To the south of Crewe station extensive goods facilities were established, together with large carriage sidings. In addition large engine sheds were built to the north and south of the town to provide locomotives to meet the increasing goods and freight requirements. The North shed, located where the Chester line left the West Coast Main Line, housed express engines and in addition heavy maintenance and repair work was carried out.

The South shed, built in the 1890s, was close to the marshalling yard and met demands for goods locomotives needed locally, as well as receiving 'visitors', including Great Western Railway (GWR) locomotives working from the West Midlands and Shrewsbury areas.

Recalling Crewe's phenomenal growth as a railway town, the *Crewe Guardian* wrote in 1887: 'Fifty years ago the place where Crewe is now located was nothing more than a small hamlet, a few labourers' cottages scattered about, and farms dotted here and there like currants in a penny bun …'.

2
North Staffordshire Lines West of Stoke-On-Trent

Keele/Audley/Alsager Road/Harecastle
Harecastle/Sandbach
Stoke/Harecastle/Crewe

Keele/Audley/Alsager Road/Harecastle

When a line from Silverdale to Market Drayton was approved on 29th July 1864, a separate branch was agreed on the same day to become known as the Audley line. It was covered by a separate Act and it included goods branches to places such as Bignall Hill, Chesterton, Grange and Jamage. The Audley line opened to industrial traffic on 24th July 1870, running from Silverdale to join the main Kidsgrove to Crewe line to the east of Alsager. Construction had been slow, particularly between Silverdale and Leycett, requiring the excavation of a deep cutting followed by a high embankment. But this section was beset throughout with problems from flooding and mining subsidence and was abandoned when an alternative, longer route became available in 1870.

There were further problems with the many colliery sidings proving sub-standard and it was to be quite a number of years before the Board of Trade approved the line for passenger traffic. Eventually it was agreed that the permanent way and the signalling met requirements, and passenger services between Stoke and Harecastle commenced on the Audley branch on 28th June 1880. Later that year, on 1st October 1880, the southern end of the branch was diverted to improve the junction with the Market Drayton line, giving an easier access to reach Stoke.

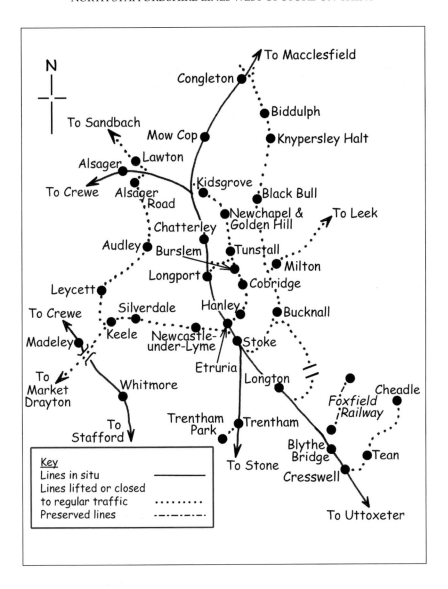

There were four trains each way daily and two on Sundays.
Intermediate stations were at Leycett, Halmerend and Audley,

The NSR Keele station in 1956 on the Stoke to Market Drayton branch. Keele also served a branch to Alsager, which carried much coal traffic. (Stations UK)

with the buildings constructed of wood for cheapness. On July 1st 1889 a fourth station opened called 'Talke & Alsager Road' but the name was shortened to Alsager Road in 1902.

On 27th April 1931 passenger services came to an end, forced to close through competition from buses, which proved more convenient. Over the next three decades, coal trains survived but they were run down as pits became worked out and continued to close. In 1969 Leycett's small station was demolished along with the rest of the village. Miners had to be re-housed in either Silverdale or Madeley. The last colliery in the area to close was at Silverdale, which came to an end on 24th December 1998. It was a sad day for around 200 miners. Some took home a piece of coal from the coalface to keep as a souvenir of times past. A

24

short section of the former track between Audley and Alsager gave way to bulldozers when a link road (A500) was constructed between the M6 and the Potteries.

Harecastle/Sandbach

Although mainly in Cheshire, this short branch emanated from Harecastle in Staffordshire and warrants mention. This NSR line of 6½ miles passing through quiet Cheshire countryside must surely have had the reputation of being one of the country's shortest-lived passenger lines. The Act agreeing the branch was passed by Parliament in 1846 but it was to be another 47 years before it opened throughout to passengers and then it lasted only 37 years. Had it developed further, it could have taken NSR trains closer to Liverpool but, as it was, it settled initially for goods traffic only from 1852, between

Sandbach station photographed in 1966. This was a busy junction in LNWR days. Apart from handling through Crewe to Manchester traffic, it also provided direct services to Northwich and (by NSR trains) to Harecastle. (Stations UK)

Hassall Green on the former NSR branch between Harecastle and Sandbach, photographed in 1948. The station closed to passengers in 1930. (Stations UK)

This is all that was left of Wheelock station when photographed in 1948 on the former NSR branch from Kidsgrove to Sandbach. The station closed in 1930 with the station building becoming a garage. The line remained open until the 1970s as a 'Crewe avoiding' line. (Stations UK)

Lawton junction (on the main Crewe/Stoke line) and Ettiley Heath, a goods depot just short of Sandbach (on the Crewe/Manchester route). When goods services reached Sandbach in 1866, the branch was seen as a useful means to take pressure off some of Crewe's freight traffic.

Passenger services commenced on 3rd July 1893 with intermediate stations at Lawton, Hassall Green and Wheelock. Between Hassall Green and Wheelock a short siding carried freight to and from Malkin's Bank, the vast alkali works of Brunner Mond, the forerunner of ICI. On 28th July 1930 passenger services on the branch came to an end but the line continued usefully carrying freight until the early 1970s as a Crewe avoiding route.

Today Harecastle station is no more. When the route from Euston to the North West was electrified in the 1960s, the nearby tunnels were found to be too narrow for present day stock. One tunnel (Harecastle North) was opened out and two others were abandoned. British Rail constructed a loop and built Harecastle station at a new site but renamed it Kidsgrove Central. When the

Kidsgrove Central station, formerly Harecastle station, in 1966. Trains left for Crewe on the left and bore right towards Macclesfield and Stockport. (Stations UK)

When electrification of the main line between Euston and the North West was completed in 1966/7, a diversion line was opened bypassing Harecastle's earlier three tunnels. This former tunnel, photographed in 1967, has been demolished. (Courtesy Staffordshire County Museum, Shugborough)

Potteries Loop line closed in 1964 Kidsgrove Central became known as Kidsgrove. Hassall Green's former station building exists as a private residence although rather overshadowed by the M6 motorway. Wheelock station building has become a garage found at the top end of the town whilst the former platform is lost in the wooded glade below.

Two useful contributions to preserved railways came from the branch. The signal box currently in use at the North Staffordshire Railway at Cheddleton came from Elton crossing at Sandbach and the signal box and crossing gates at Hassell Green found their way to Hadlow Road station museum in the Wirral Country Park, on the former Hooton to West Kirby branch.

Stoke/Harecastle/Crewe

The short 8¼ mile line from Harecastle to Crewe was originally a product of the North Staffordshire Railway (NSR), which aimed for a link between the LNWR's West Coast Main Line and Eastern England. Authorised in June 1846, the NSR soon ran into difficulties when Lord Crewe raised objections over a proposed route. As a result the NSR was compelled to submit a revised route to Parliament which required the tracks to leave the Crewe main line three miles to the south and then rejoin the originally planned route at Radway Green. This was approved by Parliament in July 1847.

Passenger and freight services began on 9th October 1848 but initially, because of disputes with the LNWR, traffic was light. Today the line carries passenger services between Crewe and Skegness via Stoke and Nottingham. The track between Crewe and Radway Green has been singled, Radway Green station

Locomotive no 45638 hauls an express at Stoke, photographed on 17th September 1958. (D.K. Jones Collection)

BR 2-6-0 locomotive no 76022 stands by shed 5D at Stoke in March 1933, awaiting duties. (D. K. Jones Collection)

A 1924 picture of former North Staffordshire Railway locomotive no 23 (seen as LMS 2367). (D. K. Jones Collection)

A North Staffordshire Railway locomotive photographed at Stoke, c1922. Stoke first appeared on a railway map in April 1848, as a temporary terminus from Norton Bridge. From that small beginning, lines soon progressed across the country (D. K. Jones Collection)

having closed in 1966. Electrification has been considered but, with inadequate support, the idea has foundered.

Alsager station, today the only intermediate station between Crewe and Kidsgrove, has survived. Earlier in 1996 the station's southern buildings and canopy, which in part date back to 1848, were saved from demolition. This is thanks to funds made available which includes a contribution from Congleton Borough Council. The buildings on the northern side have been let for community use.

A local resident who lived in the Chatterley area (north of Stoke) recalls his first family holiday back in the earlier days of steam. The journey first entailed a train to Crewe, where he says they 'changed from the severe austerity of the North Staffordshire Railway to the magnificent luxury of the London & North Western'. Another journey recalled, overnight on this occasion, was from Crewe to Aberystwyth in a gas-lit Great Western Railway coach and his 'being sick on Machynlleth station in the cold grey hours of dawn'!

3

Staffordshire Pit Lines
and a Loop

Stoke/Bucknall/Biddulph/Congleton
Bucknall/Endon/Leek
Etruria/Tunstall/Kidsgrove

Bucknall station, photographed in 1948, on the Biddulph Valley branch from Stoke to Congleton. The line closed to passengers in 1927 but continued in parts for many years, serving adjacent collieries. (Stations UK)

Stoke/Bucknall/Biddulph/Congleton

Stoke developed a national reputation for the excellence of its pottery in the 19th century although the manufacturing process was far cruder and more wasteful than in today's kilns. For each ton of clay about ten tons of coal were needed for the firing of products. Thus the siting of the Potteries, in an age of primitive transport, owed as much to the presence of nearby pits as to local clays. The area has its origins in numerous communities, which together gave plentiful employment. In the 1920s, for example, more than 4,500 men worked at Chatterley Whitfield colliery alone. Such was the power wielded by the colliery owners that they could compel smaller railway companies to build lines to carry their products where needed and, if the railway companies declined, they said they would build a railway themselves. It was in such circumstances that the Potteries, Biddulph and Congleton Railway was conceived and, when the railway company went ahead, it had to carry all the colliery's expenses!

The Biddulph Valley line from Stoke to a terminal at Congleton was agreed by Parliament on 24th July 1854. The NSR accepted a tender of £87,500 submitted by William and Solomon Tredwell and the first sod was cut on 27th April 1858. Since the movement of coal was the line's greatest priority, it commenced initially for goods only on 29th August 1860. Passenger services began on 1st June 1864, when the *Macclesfield Courier* reported: 'The first passenger train left Stoke at 8.45 am, the engine driver having decorated his iron horse with oak and laburnum, interspersed with a few flags emblazoned with the Staffordshire Knot.'

As expected, the line was busiest with mineral traffic. With Whitfield colliery producing near to a million tons annually by 1900 (it reached its first million in 1937), and with other collieries along the branch such as Northwood or Birchenwood, the line could not fail. Originally coal trains from the Chatterley Whitfield colliery joined the branch near Black Bull but when the Potteries Loop line was built, the colliery built its own system, the Whitfield Colliery Railway, joining the Loop south of Tunstall. This spur to Tunstall became known as the Pinnox branch.

Travelling the Biddulph Valley branch from Stoke, tracks left the main Stoke–Derby line to curve northwards to Fenton Manor, which was opened later in October 1889. Originally a

Black Bull station on the Bucknall/Congleton line. The line became known as the 'inner circle' of the Potteries with trains every half hour. (Stations UK)

wooden platform, a brick extension was added in May 1892. At Botteslow junction, the Longton, Adderley Green & Bucknall Railway left the main branch, diverging to the east. This was a little known but busy mineral line sanctioned in 1866 to reach Longton plus two pit branches. It was later extended to Park Hall on the main Stoke/Uttoxeter line to become a circular route. When taken over by the NSR in May 1895, the line was immediately cut in two by the abandonment of a ¼ mile stretch close to the southern end. This was done partly to simplify working and also to benefit the NSR by increasing revenue from the longer hauls required. Even though powers were granted to run passenger trains, this never happened.

Back to the Biddulph line and not far from Northwood colliery came Bucknall & Northwood station. A mile or so further north at Milton junction, trains left for Leek and Waterhouses. Before Ford Green & Smallthorne station, the track was crossed by a mineral line between Nettlebank Wharf

Congleton station, April 2005, on the main line from Kidsgrove to Macclesfield. On weekdays in the early 1920s there were six trains daily for Stoke via Leek. (Author)

and Ford Green ironworks. In 1890 Chatterley Whitfield introduced its own workmen's train with services starting from the pit yard. After Black Bull station and a private spur to Birchenwood colliery came Knypersley Halt. The name Knypersley means 'the village under the rocks' and near the busy crossroads stands the parish church of St John, donated by the Bateman family as well as coal owners and industrialists from the 19th century. Beyond Biddulph and Mossley halt, the branch passed under the main line (Congleton to Macclesfield) to its terminus at Congleton, with a spur climbing to join the main route.

When the London, Midland & Scottish Railway (LMS) took over after grouping in the early 1920s, the Biddulph branch was one of the first to suffer. The LMS thought the line had no future for passenger traffic and regular Stoke/Congleton services ended on 11th July 1927. Mineral traffic continued healthily for many years even though the industry was in decline. In 1963 the branch lost its spur at Congleton to the main line and the following year the Pinnox line closed when a new connection to the Biddulph line was installed. Further closures followed in 1968 when the line north of Biddulph closed and in 1976 between Ford Green and Biddulph (Victoria colliery). When the section between Ford Green and Milton junction went, only the line from Stoke to Milton junction survived, providing freight services beyond via Leek to Oakamoor and Caldon Low.

Bucknall/Endon/Leek

The Milton junction branch to join the Rocester to North Rode line, agreed by Parliament on 13th July 1863, was single track and over six miles in length. There were delays in completion since considerable earthworks were necessary and there were also difficulties in raising the necessary finance. Over four years after authorisation, on 1st November 1867, the line finally opened to both passenger and freight traffic.

There were intermediate stations at Milton, Stockton Brook, Endon and Wall Grange. At Stockton Brook the railway line still passes diagonally under a crossroads that includes the busy A53 from Stoke to Leek. The next stop eastwards was Endon where the platform has survived, a shop standing today on the site of the platform building. A section of the Caldon Canal passes Endon but at a height of 490 ft above sea level. Built by James Brindley in 1777, it is believed to be the highest canal in Britain. It is no longer used commercially but following restoration by the Caldon Canal Society and British Waterways, it brings much pleasure as a leisure cruiseway.

The railway lasted until 7th May 1956 when passenger services from Stoke to Leek were withdrawn. The line remained in use for goods linking Stoke with Oakamoor and Caldon Low and, for a time from 1956 to 1960, the branch was used by football specials. Although the track remains today, it is no longer in use although the section between Cheddleton and Kingsley & Froghall has reopened and is in use today with trains from the preserved Cheddleton Railway Centre (Chapter 5).

Leek station, c1930, where a short branch from Bucknall reached the Rocester to North Rode line. Following the station's final closure to passengers and freight in 1970, the buildings were demolished to make way for a supermarket. (Stations UK)

Etruria/Tunstall/Kidsgrove

'The formal death announcement of the historic Potteries Loop Line passenger service was issued by British Railways today. Only the date of the execution – method the Beeching Axe – remains to be fixed.' The above statement headed a newspaper feature in January 1964. Another reported: 'The death knell sounded for the line some time ago and many of its daytime services have already been suspended. But when the Minister's official approval of the closure came last week, it caused bitterness and strong protests among the many regulars who use the half-a-dozen daily trains.' The Potteries Loop Line always had a place in NSR ('Knotty') supporters' hearts and such was the reaction locally when the London Midland Region headquarters at Birmingham announced its closure.

To go back to its beginning, several Acts required Parliamentary approval before the Loop line through the heavily populated and industrial areas to the east of Stoke could be completed. A goods line had already reached Hanley in December 1861 and it was to be another four years before the NSR received approval to complete the line from Hanley via Burslem and Tunstall to Kidsgrove. Meantime industry had slumped and the NSR was anxious to abandon the idea. Local feeling in favour of the line ran high and an approach by the NSR to Parliament to give up the Loop was rejected. To cut costs the NSR investigated a narrow gauge system but this proposal was thrown out by shareholders.

Construction went ahead with the first sod cut on 21st July 1870 at Burslem with John Watkin, the town's Chief Bailiff, officiating. In his book *The Potteries Loop Line*, Allan C. Baker wrote that much celebration followed and the guests, no doubt accompanied by many others, repaired to the Leopard Hotel for suitable refreshments. By all accounts a good time was had by all. Over five years later, on 15th November 1875, the Loop line finally opened as a through route from Etruria to Kidsgrove. The *Staffordshire*

Trains left the main Stoke to Harecastle line at Etruria for the Potteries Loop line to Kidsgrove. The line opened in 1875 for freight and passengers but closed in 1964 despite much bitterness and local opposition. (Stations UK)

Daily Sentinel reported: 'There was a great stir in consequence of the opening of this line, so much so, that it was observed to be very much like the Wakes and many of the pits were idle. The first two trains were very much crowded, while a still greater number surrounded the entrance to the [Kidsgrove] station.'

The first full passenger service came into operation in 1875 with as many as 25 trains each way on weekdays from Tunstall southwards via Stoke to Longton or Blythe Bridge. Initially only a few trains travelled northwards from Tunstall towards Kidsgrove where demand was less. The Loop line became known as the 'inner circle' of the Potteries and with trains every half hour, the NSR, despite its earlier forebodings, found the branch very profitable. The trains, mostly older four-wheeled coaches hauled by 2-4-0 side tank locomotives known as 'Sharp Tanks', carried special name boards with 'Loop Line Train' in black letters on a white background. After a few years some of the four-wheeled coaches were replaced by six-wheeled carriages.

In 1909 a halt was opened at Kidsgrove to encourage traffic. A disadvantage for Loop traffic was the lack of any direct connection with Harecastle station on the main Stoke/Macclesfield line. When trains at the northern end of the Loop joined the main Macclesfield line they were beyond Harecastle station and facing the wrong direction. Plans were considered to overcome this but nothing was ever done.

On 1st July 1923 the NSR became part of the London, Midland & Scottish Railway (LMS). Changes were inevitable, particularly with competition from buses already affecting Loop traffic. Even so by the late 1920s, there were still some 20 trains daily between Tunstall and Stoke. Some extended northwards to terminate at either Kidsgrove or Congleton, while southwards trains went to Blythe Bridge, Cheadle or Uttoxeter. Just prior to the Second World War (1939–1945) some Sunday trains ran to and from Trentham Park, a terminus on a short one mile branch close to Trentham Gardens. In October 1944 Harecastle station on the main line was renamed Kidsgrove Central and Kidsgrove station on the loop became Kidsgrove London Road. After closure of the loop Kidsgrove Central became just Kidsgrove.

As pits closed over the years that followed, freight traffic reduced considerably. Closure to passenger services came on 2nd March 1964 although short sections survived for a number of years for freight purposes. Meantime electrification of the main line between Euston and the North West was in hand and a Harecastle tunnel diversion line was opened on 27th June 1966. This was necessary because the original main line tunnels were too narrow for the new trains. Harecastle North tunnel (130 yds) was opened out and the Middle (180 yds) and South (1,763 yds) tunnels were abandoned. Today only a 220 yd tunnel is required. When a full electric service began on 2nd January 1967, track lifting along the Loop was put in hand.

After more than a century the Loop line may be no more but it is still remembered by many. Today much of the trackbed has become a pathway known as the Loop Greenway. At the site where the Pitt's Hill section was opened in 1972, a set of class 5 standard driving wheels have been set in a concrete bed.

A reminder of the former Loop line. Driving wheels (class 5 standard) set in concrete, can be found today at Pitt's Hill on the pathway known as Loop Greenway. (Author)

40

4

A Restored Colliery Line, Two Branches and an Interesting Pub

The Foxfield Steam Railway
Cresswell/Cheadle
Trentham/Trentham Park
The Spot Gate Inn, near Stone

Blythe Bridge station, c1947, on the NSR Uttoxeter to Stoke line. The line survives today but the cast iron columns saved from the original Blythe Bridge station building can now be seen at the Foxfield Railway's Caverswall Road station. (Stations UK)

The Foxfield Steam Railway

A visit to the Foxfield Steam Railway at Blythe Bridge can also be a trip back into history. In the late 1880s a shaft was sunk in Foxfield Wood and the resultant colliery was named after it. Initially most of the coal was taken by narrow gauge railway to the outskirts of Cheadle, but as coal production increased, a standard gauge freight line was built to connect with the NSR line at Blythe Bridge. The line was built with the minimum of earthworks, hence the steep gradients and sharp curves found at the Foxfield today.

When the colliery closed in August 1965 the site was purchased by a consortium of local companies with plans to process various minerals for the nearby pottery industry and it was expected that the rail link to the Uttoxeter to Stoke line at Blythe Bridge would prove useful. This did not happen but fortunately some of the directors of one of the companies, Tean Minerals Ltd, showed interest in preserving the line. In 1967 the Foxfield Light Railway Society was formed and Tean Minerals generously gave the society unrestricted use of the line plus certain of the buildings and sidings.

Today steam-hauled trains provide a regular service from Caverswall Road on Sundays and Bank Holidays from Easter to the end of September when it is possible to enjoy a five mile journey through unspoilt countryside. The railway is home to numerous steam, diesel and electric locomotives along with a wide variety of coaches and freight vehicles, many of which can be seen at the Caverswall Road station headquarters, Blythe Bridge, Stoke-on-Trent. Unfortunately many of these had to be delivered by road transport, since in the mid-1970s BR, for reasons best known to itself, removed the connection with the main line. Within the last decade a locomotive running shed has been completed named the Hollick Building after the late Jack Hollick, a founder member and former President of the Foxfield Railway.

Today the enthusiasm of volunteers at Foxfield is hard to match. Trains run from Caverswall Road station to Dilhorne Park and back. Thanks to a Lottery Heritage Grant, winding gear and other buildings have been acquired from the former

The driver of 'Meaford No 2' picks up a token after leaving Caverswall Road station at the Foxfield Railway. (Photograph courtesy Mark Smith)

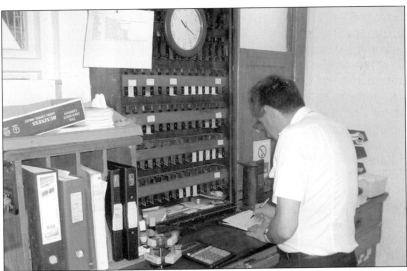

The ticket rack and booking office desk at today's Blythe Bridge (Caverswall Road) on the preserved Foxfield Railway came from Gnosall station on the Wellington to Stafford branch. (Photo courtesy Ian Rutherford)

colliery. It is hoped that by the year 2007 a Mining Village Centre will be opened. It will be reached by extending the track a further ¾ mile, part of which will include a 1 in 19 gradient.

Relics from earlier days can also be found. In Caverswall Road station building, parts of the wooden booking office originally came from Gnosall, previously on the Wellington to Stafford line. The station frontage includes cast iron columns saved from the original Blythe Bridge station on the main line. A bonus for many is perhaps that the station has added a bar that specialises in real ale on handpull.

When the author paid a visit to Caverswall Road, he was privileged to have a footplate ride on steam-powered 0-6-0 Hunslet, works no 3694, acquired by Steve Turner in 1983. After working Lancashire collieries, it has seen many travels. When the author subsequently rejoined his wife, herself a rail enthusiast some of the time, instead of acclamations of praise and envy, her only comment was, 'Your hands are dirty!'

Cresswell/Cheadle

There were great celebrations when a crowded first train left Totmonslow (Tean from December 1906) via Cresswell for Tunstall on the Potteries Loop line on 7th November 1892. Hauled by an NSR tank locomotive, Cheadle branch trains were to become an extension of Loop line services. But the celebrations could be considered somewhat premature, for another eight years were to pass before trains actually reached Cheadle.

A branch to Cheadle was first considered in the early 1850s when the local people felt they had been neglected by the Stoke–Uttoxeter and the Churnet Valley lines, which passed nearly four miles each side of the town. Various ideas were proposed and rejected and it was not until August 1888 that Parliament agreed a line. The townsfolk of Cheadle, having waited so many years, were impatient to get their railway and the first sod was cut on 22nd March 1888, five months before the Bill was passed.

Cresswell station, c1948, on the main Stoke to Uttoxeter line. It was from Cresswell that the branch to Cheadle opened in 1901. It was a difficult line to construct with a tunnel of 977 yds and with gradients reaching 1 in 40. (Stations UK)

Many problems were to follow before the line was completed. As the company ran out of money, so work stopped. In addition a costly tunnel 977 yds long was required with gradients reaching 1 in 40. Trains eventually reached Cheadle on 1st January 1901, some 13 years after Parliamentary approval had been given. There were five trains each way daily and two on Sundays, still an extension of the Loop line traffic. Freight traffic was spasmodic, dependent on the output of the two collieries, Draycott and New Haden, along the route. Almost from the start there was a problem with the tunnel when part of the lining collapsed and repairs proved a heavy expense. When the two collieries closed during 1906, finances further deteriorated and the Cheadle Railway Company went into liquidation.

Matters improved when the NSR took over in 1907. Services increased, the New Haden colliery reopened under new ownership and Tean acquired a more permanent station building. Passengers had to wait another two years before toilets were opened! A cottage near the station served as a booking office, a building which survives as a private residence. At Cheadle a large new station with an awning was built plus a large house for the station-master. This awning would have proved useful at Foxfield's Caverswall Road station but BR demolished it along with the station after closure.

Troubles with the tunnel persisted, much of it caused by the New Haden colliery workings. Events took a dramatic turn on a Sunday afternoon on 2nd November 1918 when 400 ft of the tunnel roof at the Cheadle end collapsed, completely blocking the line. Fortunately no trains were running at the time and traffic was suspended for several weeks while extensive repairs were carried out.

When in 1923 the LMS took over control of the NSR and with it the Cheadle branch, it also inherited the continuing tunnel problem. Troubles persisted and in 1931 Parliament agreed that a diversion line could be built skirting the high ground. Work

A DMU waits for return from Cheadle station (photographed c1959). Cheadle is the terminus for a short branch from the main Stoke to Uttoxeter line. The station closed in 1963 and was demolished in the last few years to make way for private homes. (Stations UK)

46

A general view of Cheadle station and goods yard taken in 1963. In earlier steam days, passengers changed at Cresswell on the main Stoke–Uttoxeter line for Cheadle. Four trains ran each way daily. (Stations UK)

This is all that remains of Cheadle station today. The station-master's house above the former station area still survives as a private residence. (Author)

began in 1932, which included the removal of some 145,000 cubic yards of earth. Finally after over 30 years of problems the new line was opened on 26th November 1933. In his book *The Cheadle Railway*, Allan C. Baker rightly asks why was the line not initially built to skirt the high ground? How too could the LMS justify such a heavy financial outlay on a relatively unimportant branch?

Traffic declined during the Second World War with further losses in 1943 when New Haden colliery closed. There was some compensation when a small brickworks was installed near the colliery site, providing useful goods traffic for the movement of staple sand. Nationalisation followed in 1948 and in 1953 Tean station closed through lack of use. Despite falling traffic generally, passenger traffic survived until 1963. The last train, the 5.07 pm from Cheadle, ran on Saturday, 17th June 1963. Fifteen years later public freight workings were withdrawn.

Cheadle station site can be found along Station Road. All that remains is the station-master's house, currently a private residence. The station building has been demolished to make

Tean, set in a deep cutting, was the only intermediate station on the Cheadle branch. The former station site is difficult to trace today with the line almost totally overgrown. (Author)

way for a bungalow. Tean platform is still there but cannot be seen due to an overgrown and neglected track. It is situated in a cutting below a bridge on a minor road from Upper Tean to Longton. But no trains pass – only the ghosts of ex-LMS class 5 or class 8 or perhaps an Ivatt 2-6-0 might be heard.

Trentham/Trentham Park

The 1,000 acres of Trentham Gardens to the south of Stoke-on-Trent have a long and colourful history dating back to Saxon times. During the 19th century the estate was the ancestral home of the Dukes of Sutherland. Today the area offers a wide range of activities ranging from clay pigeon shooting or water skiing, to a wildfowl reserve or a children's funfair. Also included is a miniature railway, but standard gauge trains travelled the 1¼ mile branch that opened to the gardens in April 1910.

Even though Trentham Gardens were within walking distance from the main line station of Trentham, the NSR decision to build this short branch justified itself. But plans to extend by constructing the Trentham, Newcastle-under-Lyme and Silverdale Railway to form a western outer circle around Stoke came to nothing when the First World War broke out in 1914. All that was built was a steel girder bridge on high brick abutments (all now demolished) beyond the Trentham Gardens terminus over the A34.

The branch had only one intermediate stop – at Hanford Road Halt, today hardly a rural area. The halt closed in 1913 but the branch itself lasted until a few days after the Second World War began, closing to regular passenger traffic on 11th September 1939. Excursion traffic continued for a time but the line closed completely in October 1957.

The Spot Gate Inn, near Stone

Interesting railway relics can be found at the Spot Gate public house to the north of Hilderstone and near Stone where two

A freight train passes through Trentham station on the main NSR line between Stoke and Stone. From Trentham a 1¼ mile branch was built to Trentham Park. Plans to extend the line to create a loop west of Stoke came to nothing and the branch closed to regular passenger traffic in 1939. (Stations UK)

Looking southwards at Stone station where lines divided to either Stafford or Rugeley and Lichfield. Not far away, near Hilderstone, can be found the Spot Gate Inn where two Pullman coaches serve as part of the restaurant. (Stations UK)

An early LNER notice, displayed in the Spot Gate Inn, warning that 'all persons' who dare to trespass on company property would be liable to 'fine or imprisonment'. (Author)

Car no 75 at the Spot Gate Inn worked with the Golden Arrow in 1960 as well as the Bournemouth Belle from 1965 to 1967. (Author)

Inside one of the Pullman Restaurant cars at the Spot Gate Inn where meals are served to a high standard in evocative surroundings. (Author)

'retired' coaches form the popular Pullman Restaurant. The coaches have quite a history, with one named *Ursula*, a parlour 1st class, being one of 30 made to introduce the Queen of Scots service that remained with the London & North Eastern Railway (LNER) until the early 1960s. After service with the Bournemouth Belle, it was withdrawn in 1967.

The second coach had the added distinction that it worked with the Golden Arrow in 1960 as well as the Bournemouth Belle from 1965 to 1967. Both were built by the Metropolitan Carriage Wagon & Finance Co of Saltley, Birmingham in 1928 and after withdrawal were sold to Allied Breweries. Today it is possible to enjoy a fine meal in either coach and, at the same time, capture much of the railway spirit of the past.

5

The Churnet Valley Branch, a Line into Derbyshire and Steam at Cheddleton

Uttoxeter/Leek/North Rode
Rocester/Ashbourne/Parsley Hay
The Cheddleton Railway Centre

Locomotive class 9F no 92203 'Black Prince' emerges in summer 2004 from the 462 yd Leek Brook tunnel between Cheddleton and Leek Brook junction. (Photograph courtesy D.R. Gibson)

Uttoxeter/Leek/North Rode

The North Staffordshire Railway (NSR) line from Uttoxeter to North Rode could well have achieved far greater importance, for it provided the shortest distance between Euston and Manchester. Although used by some through services, most of the trains ran via Stoke or Crewe. When it opened on 13th July 1849, there were initially four trains each way daily with two on Sundays but equally important was the branch's freight traffic. Milk from the Churnet, Dane and Dove areas left regularly for London or Manchester and copper transported from Oakamoor and later from Froghall proved profitable.

Powers to build the Churnet Valley Railway were granted in 1846. At the time two other companies were planning lines in Staffordshire: the Potteries and the Harecastle & Sandbach. These combined in 1847 to become the North Staffordshire Railway. Although the Churnet Valley branch was completed in three years, it was not easy to construct. Part of the track

Locomotives stabled in Uttoxeter engine shed. In its heyday Uttoxeter was a busy junction. Today there is no trace of the engine shed. (Stations UK)

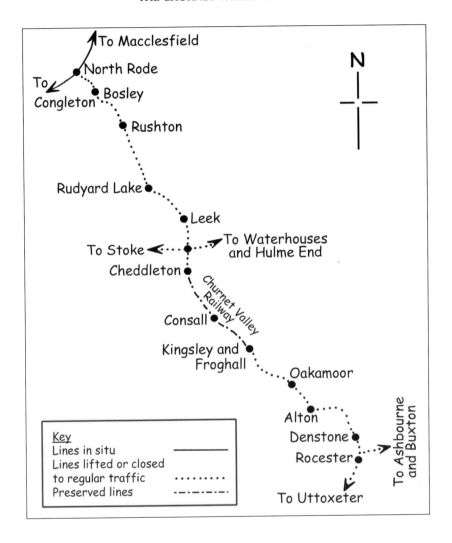

between Froghall and Uttoxeter had to be laid on a drained canal and in addition four tunnels had to be bored. Leek and Alton were considered to be the main intermediate stations and the 'clerks' in charge received a higher salary than their colleagues at the lesser stops. In an NSR Rule Book of the day, staff were expected to ensure that 'all servants came on duty clean in their persons and their clothes, shaved and with their shoes blacked'. Later the shaving rule was relaxed for engine drivers, who were allowed to grow beards, presumably to serve as chest protectors!

Travelling southwards from North Rode, the line passed through pleasant countryside to reach Bosley, a timber-style station set in a cutting. Next came Rushton where the station building survives today as an attractive private residence. A prominent notice on the wall reads BEWARE OF TRAINS. Rudyard Lake station (opened in 1905) came next, known as Cliffe Park from 1926. The lake was created as a reservoir for the Caldon Canal. It was at this lakeside that Stoke architect Kipling proposed to Rudyard Kipling's mother and later the name of the location was given to the famous novelist and poet.

At the south end of the lake came Rudyard (Horton) station, which was known as Rudyard Lake prior to 1905. It seems hard to believe that not too many years ago, on Bank Holidays, trains ran from Leek to Rudyard and back every quarter of an hour. Leek was reached after crossing the river Churnet and passing through the 462 yd Leek tunnel. Today all trace of the station has gone and the site is occupied by a supermarket. To the south was Leek Brook Halt, opened at the turn of the century to serve a newly built mental hospital. The halt had one platform plus a bay which accommodated an electrically powered branch to the hospital for freight and visitors although later it was for freight only.

Cheddleton station, sited some way from the village of the same name, possessed a small siding hardly adequate to cope with the output of a nearby paper mill. Consall opened in 1902 serving a small community, followed by Kingsley & Froghall, which became an important rail point. Nearby was the terminus of the Caldon Canal and the tramway from the Caldon Quarries. In the book *The Churnet Valley Railway*, R. Keys writes that a signal box just to the north of Kingsley & Froghall station was staffed for many years by an unfortunate fellow who lost both legs when he was run over by a train. The NSR provided him with wooden stumps and kept him in his employment where he became affectionately known as 'Peg-Leg' Johnson.

A local train awaits departure at Alton Towers station, c1959. The station was used by the Earl of Shrewsbury and it had a goods lift to raise the Earl's baggage to road level. (Stations UK)

Alton Towers station building is today a strictly private residence. The station was in a deep cutting and passengers had to negotiate many steps. (Author)

Kingsley & Froghall station in 1948, which closed to passenger traffic in 1965. Today the station is fully restored being the southern terminus of the Churnet Valley Railway. (Stations UK)

Oakamoor gained its reputation from the local industries sited in the area. One of the most important was the copper business of Thomas Bolton & Sons, which produced the first successful transatlantic cable. To the south, Alton station building, which was built in a style to match Alton Towers, former home of the Earl of Shrewsbury, survives today and is listed. Situated on the steep side of the Churnet Valley, the station had a luggage lift to hoist the Earl's belongings up to his front entrance. Excursion trains to Alton were many and a long bay platform coped with the busy traffic. In the 1920s Alton Towers estate was sold to a local consortium, which opened a pleasure park, a feature that it very much remains today.

The last intermediate station before Rocester was Denstone, built originally to serve the Heywood family who lived in what became Denstone College. It had a very low platform and passengers had to alight down small step-ladders provided for the purpose. At Rocester the branch joined the line from Ashbourne, thus completing almost 28 miles of delightful

Denstone station, c1923, between Uttoxeter and Leek. It was built originally to serve the Heywood family who lived in what became Denstone College. (Stations UK)

Rocester station, photographed in 1957. Trains left Rocester for Leek, or via Ashbourne to Parsley Hay in Derbyshire. Following closure in 1965, the station was demolished to become a vast JCB excavator works. (Station UK)

scenery. Today the site of Rocester station has become a vast JCB excavator works and some locals have claimed that at night 'ghosts trains' can still be heard in the factory buildings.

The North Rode to Leek section closed to passengers in November 1960 and Leek to Uttoxeter followed in January 1965. Freight continued for a time but in November 1992 even the lines that still exist from Stoke via Leek Brook junction to Oakamoor and Caldon Low were no longer in use. Is it possible perhaps that one day Tarmac or Redland freight trains may travel the line again?

Looking back, it seems incredible that in 1973 Leek Urban Council failed to see any potential in bringing steam back between Leek and Rudyard Lake despite petitions from many Leek residents for the line to be preserved. It seems even more incredible a town the size of Leek, has no railway at all!

In 1985 trains did return to Rudyard but with a 10¼ in gauge layout along part of the former trackbed. Services run most summer weekends and occasionally on weekdays during school

Rudyard Lake Railway locomotive 'Excalibur', one of the several diesel and steam engines that haul coaches along a 3 mile round trip on 10¼ in gauge track alongside the attractive Rudyard Lake. (Author)

holidays. The privately owned system includes three locomotives, *Kingsley*, an 0-4-0 diesel powered, an 0-4-0 petrol engine and *Ivanhoe*, a 4-4-0 steam, as well as numerous open bogie coaches.

Consultants have suggested there is potential in reopening the existing track from Stoke, via Leek, to Oakamoor and providing an extension to Alton, which would serve the leisure park. Yet part of this has already seen a return to services with trains from the Cheddleton Railway Centre running between Cheddleton and Kingsley & Froghall.

Rocester/Ashbourne/Parsley Hay

The seven mile NSR branch from Rocester to Ashbourne in Derbyshire, which opened in 1852, carried little traffic although this improved when the LNWR opened its branch from Buxton to

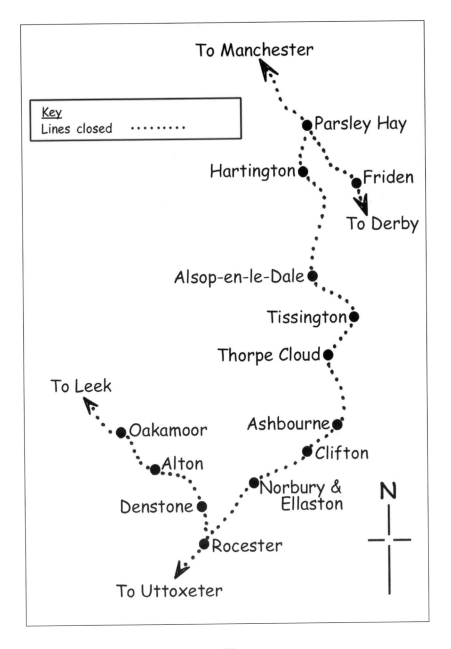

To Manchester

Key
Lines closed · · · · · · · ·

Parsley Hay

Hartington Friden

To Derby

Alsop-en-le-Dale

Tissington

Thorpe Cloud

To Leek

Oakamoor Ashbourne

Alton Clifton

Denstone Norbury &
Ellaston

N

Rocester

To Uttoxeter

Ashbourne in 1899, nearly 50 years later. The through route now possible was considered as yet another alternative for services from Euston to Manchester but this did not happen, since the mileage was 194 compared with 183½ via Crewe. The branch was never brought up to main line standard even though the NSR section was doubled when LNWR services from Buxton began.

A day or so before the LNWR line opened, the villagers of Hartington in Derbyshire were given free rides to Ashbourne, some of them never having travelled on a train before. For many people, particularly in bad weather, the branch became a lifeline for, when road traffic came to a standstill, the trains usually got through. Ashbourne's first station, built by the NSR in 1852, was a fine stately building of brick and stone. When the LNWR branch from Buxton arrived, it was relegated to become part of the goods depot and the new Ashbourne station was almost entirely wooden. The platforms consisted of planking which passengers found dangerous when wet.

The NSR branch's two intermediate stations were at Norbury & Ellaston and at Clifton with the track following the attractive Dove Valley along the Derbyshire border. There were four trains each way daily on weekdays, two of these later carrying through coaches to Buxton. As rail traffic dwindled in the early 1950s, a typical through train would be a couple of non-corridor coaches hauled by an LMS 2-6-4 tank locomotive. The villagers liked their railway and when closure was threatened local people demanded it should continue. The entire line closed officially to passengers on 1st November 1954 but emergency winter services were continued for a number of years.

The line finally closed to all traffic in June 1964 and the track was removed the same year. During demolition a number of wagons broke loose, to run away smashing three sets of level crossing gates almost as if in protest at the closure. Norbury & Ellaston station building has become a private residence. When visited the owner recounted how his late father travelled on the last steam and the last diesel train to Ashbourne. At Clifton, the station building has become a private residence with the former goods yard in use as a depot. At Ashbourne the station gave way to become a doctor's surgery and a swimming pool.

66

Ashbourne station's former goods depot is today in commercial use. All signs of the LNWR station have gone. The area has become a medical centre. (Author)

Although not in Staffordshire the LNWR line from Ashbourne towards Parsley Hay through part of the delightful Derbyshire Peak District is worth another brief mention. It is perhaps better known today as the Tissington Trail, the 13 mile scenic route established along the old railway trackbed. Construction had been difficult since the route included a steep climb to reach a summit of 1,250 ft above sea level. In addition a tunnel had to be bored under Ashbourne and foundations were needed for a viaduct at Hand Dale near Hartington. There are stories that when these foundations were dug, skeletons of men were found who had been trapped in old mine workings.

A walk along the Tissington Trail today can bring back many reminders of those earlier days. At Hartington a signal box survives with its levers intact but with light refreshments available at a lower level.

Ashbourne, c1910. Ashbourne's first station, built by the NSR in 1852, was a fine stately building of brick and stone. When an LNWR branch from Buxton arrived in 1894, the building was relegated to become part of the goods depot, with the new Ashbourne station almost entirely wooden. (Stations UK)

An LNWR freight train approaches Alsop-en-le-Dale station, c1963, on the Ashbourne to Parsley Hay branch in Derbyshire. The station closed to regular traffic in 1964 and has been completely demolished. (Stations UK)

At the former Hartington station on the Ashbourne to Buxton line only the signal box survives. The site is on the 13-mile long Tissington Trail, a scenic route established along the old railway trackbed. (Author)

The Cheddleton Railway Centre

In May 1974 a parish councillor passed the former Cheddleton station on his way to work and happened to notice that demolition work was in hand. Hurried negotiations with the County Council followed, with the result that the building was saved and the way became clear for the newly-formed volunteer-run North Staffordshire Railway Society, currently known as the North Staffordshire Railway Company (1978) Ltd, to establish the buildings as a headquarters and museum.

Cheddleton station, built 1847 and opened 1849, stands on the now-disused Leek Brook to Oakamoor freight line. While this line remains silent, the Cheddleton Railway Centre has by contrast gone from strength to strength. When visited by the author in May 2005, all was activity. Austerity locomotive 0-6-0T

Consall station, on the Cheddlestone Railway, has been successfully rebuilt to its original 1902 design. It reopened to the public for the first time in 50 years over the railway's 2005 '1940s weekend'. (Photograph courtesy D.R. Gibson)

no 68030, built by Hunslet in 1952, was in full steam, hauling coaches carrying many fascinated visitors between Cheddleton and Kingsley & Froghall with a brief stop at Consall. The station at Consall replaces the original, removed by BR in the 1960s, and has been successfully built to the original 1902 design. It reopened to the public for the first time in 50 years over the railway's 2005 '1940s weekend'.

The NSR signal box at Cheddleton came from Elton Crossing, near Sandbach, and the crossing box came from the Clifton station on the former Rocester to Ashbourne line. The former weighbridge office still stands and the NSR Silverdale waiting room shelter has been relocated, brick by brick, to Cheddleton. Perhaps the finest modern building is the three-road brick locomotive display hall – well worth a visit.

Kingsley & Froghall station in 2005. The Victorian tea room has been refurbished in a grand style. It is also licensed for marriages! (Author)

For young couples visiting the Cheddlestone Railway Centre there's what might be considered an unexpected bonus. All three stations are currently licensed for marriages and each one with something different to offer – from Cheddleton, to 'sleepy Consall' set deep in the heart of the Churnet Valley or to Kingsley & Froghall with its award-winning tea room, a true Victorian country station. Weddings with caterers, marquees and steam train rides are all a possibility. What an idyllic place to say 'I do'!

6
A Branch To Waterhouses And Narrow Gauge Up The Manifold Valley

Leek/Waterhouses
Waterhouses/Hulme End

A Rail Tour takes railway enthusiasts to Caldon Low Quarry in 1957. During its existence, the quarry produced some 45,000 tonnes of limestone. (Stations UK)

Leek/Waterhouses

According to the *Leek Post and Times*, a dance was held in a large tent at Waterhouses on Tuesday, 3rd October 1899. The tickets

74

were 6d each and it was expected that it would be 'lighted throughout by the New Acetylene Gas'. The occasion formed part of the programme to celebrate the cutting of the first sod for the Leek, Caldon & Waterhouses Railway. Earlier in the day, His Grace the Duke of Devonshire KG had honoured the occasion and during the ceremony a special wheelbarrow and spade were presented. A public luncheon followed with tickets at 2s 6d each.

Construction of the NSR standard gauge Waterhouses branch met many difficulties. The delays were unfortunate since the Leek & Manifold Valley Light Railway (L&MVLR) opened in June 1904 and the NSR found it necessary to acquire a bus to temporarily connect Leek and Waterhouses until its line was ready. The bus was steam operated and was purchased from Strakers for £700.

Despite appalling weather, a number of people turned out at Waterhouses when the village was eventually reached from

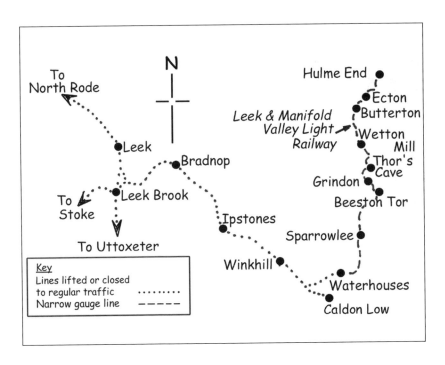

Leek on 1st July 1905. Everywhere was decorated with flags and evergreen to mark the event despite the fact that the station was not yet complete. Initially, three trains ran each way daily, comprising mixed passenger and goods, and linking with trains on the L&MVLR. Passengers could now travel directly by rail from Leek or Stoke, via Leek Brook junction, to the Manifold Valley.

Freight traffic from Caldon Quarry began in July 1906 and became an important feature of the branch, with limestone workings beginning in earnest in December 1909. Previously this had been carried by an NSR narrow gauge tramway to Froghall on the Churnet Valley line and for a time this arrangement continued. Aware of the new standard gauge

A former weigh plate house beside redundant track at Caldon Quarry. Before the standard gauge trains arrived, minerals were carried by tramway to Froghall. (Author)

service, a further quarry face was opened at Caldon requiring almost four tons of gunpowder to release some 45,000 tons of limestone.

Between Leek Brook junction and Waterhouses, principal intermediate stations were at Bradnop and Ipstones, with halts at Winkhill and Caldon Low. All were some distance from the villages they claimed to serve and as a result passenger traffic was low. By the 1920s the number of passengers had reduced even further and there was no surprise when services ended on 30th September 1935 with hardly a protest. Freight trains to Waterhouses continued for a further eight years, with 4-6-0s of Stanier class 5 or 2-8-0s of class 8 a familiar sight. After closure, the line to Caldon Quarry remained open for mineral traffic but today it is no longer in use.

With the track still in situ, the line was easy to trace by the author in 1992. Ipstones station building had gone but the broken-up platform edge had survived. At Winkhill, the

Bradnop station, c1954, on the standard gauge branch from Leek to Waterhouses. The branch opened in July 1905 to connect with the L&MVLR at Waterhouses, which had commenced services a year earlier. (Stations UK)

77

Waterhouses station in 1954 at the end of the branch from Leek. The branch closed to passengers in 1935. (Stations UK)

platform building has become a private residence. Perhaps the most nostalgic find was near the end of the quarry line at Caldon where a weigh plate house still existed by the track. A fading notice read, 'Drivers must not back their train over the weighbridge plate'.

Waterhouses/Hulme End

The former trackbed of the Leek & Manifold Valley Light Railway (L&MVLR) is today a made-up footpath and, should you wish to cycle its length, then you could well be hiring your bicycle from what was once the NSR goods shed at Waterhouses. The nearby passenger station has long since been demolished but the timber goods shed, which came from Fenton station in 1906, survives as a shop and cycle-hire point. Another distinctive reminder of the past is the 164 yd-long Swainsley

78

A mixed train, c1905. The first two wagons are on a special transporter used for carrying standard gauge stock. (Lens of Sutton)

tunnel to the south of Butterton. Today used by single line motor traffic, it is said this was built at the insistence of Sir Thomas Wardle, an L&MVLR director, so that the view from nearby Swainsley Hall should not be spoilt.

A further tangible reminder of the L&MVLR is at the northern terminus, Hulme End, where the former locomotive shed became part of a council maintenance depot. The former booking office and waiting room has also survived although the projecting canopy has gone. Not far away is the Manifold Valley Hotel where many old railway pictures are displayed. Once called the Light Railway Hotel, it was one of three owned by the NSR.

The 2 ft 6 in single track railway, nearly nine miles in length, had its official opening on Monday, 27th June 1904. As already mentioned, the rail link between Leek and Waterhouses came later, in July 1905, and local residents, well aware of this delay,

Wetton Mill station in the Manifold Valley. (Lens of Sutton)

organised a large sign to be included in the celebrations, reading 'Hurry up North Stafford'. The opening ceremony for the L&MVLR was carried out by the Earl of Dartmouth, Lord Lieutenant of the County of Stafford, after which a train, comprising two carriages and two trucks fitted with temporary seats, took Lord Dartmouth and the invited guests on 'an exceedingly pleasant journey'.

The L&MVLR possessed just two locomotives during its existence. Both 2-6-4Ts, built by Kitson & Co in 1904, they were nos 1 and 2, named ER Calthrop and JB Earle and purchased for £1,725 each. Four tramway-type bogie coaches were used, each with a length of 42 ft. Perhaps most surprising was the fact that 8 ft wide coaches were used on a 2 ft 6 in gauge track and, in order to do this, special agreement had to be given by the Board of Trade. The coaches had colonial-type end platforms and were fitted with large side windows so that passengers could enjoy the delightful scenery along the valley.

80

Locomotive 2-6-4T no 2 'JB Earle' in LMS black hauling L&MVLR coaches.
(Lens of Sutton)

Unhappily the L&MVLR was never able to build up any worthwhile freight business and, with almost total reliance on passenger traffic, it could not survive indefinitely and finances suffered. A proposed extension to Buxton might have saved the day but this was opposed by the NSR as well as local landowners. The LNWR were also uninterested and the scheme, which had lingered for many years, had to be dropped. Equally, a proposal from the L&MVLR directors that the NSR should purchase the line proved unsuccessful. For a time during the First World War, the line played an important role with the carriage of large quantities of milk in 17 gallon churns.

After the war the line suffered along with others from coal and railway strikes and the increase in competition from road transport. In January 1923 both the NSR and the L&MVLR became part of the London, Midland & Scottish Railway (LMS) following 'grouping' of railway companies into four main areas. Yet despite seasonal tourist traffic, the LMS had little interest in

The locomotive 'ER Calthrop' engaged in demolition work on the L&MVLR. The line closed in March 1934. (Lens of Sutton)

this comparatively unknown route. With the line losing money, the LMS announced that services would end on Monday, 12th March 1934.

The last train ran on Saturday, 10th March, with few supporters turning up for a final ride. The weather was cold and misty with both Leek and Waterhouses under 3 inches of snow. Within a few years, the locomotives and coaches had been scrapped and the track lifted. In the 1970s a plan was put forward to revive a section of the railway but there was much controversy. Waterhouses Secondary School announced plans to build a 10½ in gauge replica between Grindon and Wetton. Protesters including ramblers were concerned that the valley was already congested during summer weekends. One protester suggested Blackpool might be a better place for such a scheme. Despite an opinion poll recording 98% support from the local people, the Peak Planning Board rejected the plan and the railway was launched instead at Rudyard Lake between Leek and North Rode (Chapter 5).

Walkers enjoy strolling through Swainsley tunnel on the former Leek &
Manifold Railway in August 1988. (John H. Meredith)

The former L&MVLR station building at Hulme End, the northern terminus
of the line, photographed in August 1988. (John H. Meredith)

83

The former goods shed at Waterhouses is today a cycle store from where bikers can enjoy touring the attractive Manifold Valley. (Author)

The only saving grace was the purchase of the trackbed and bridges by the Staffordshire County Council, which spent £6,000 in converting the route into a footpath and bridleway. At least in such a way, visitors could continue to enjoy the delights of the beautiful Manifold Valley. What a terrible shame the line did not last until enthusiasts might have acquired the line to provide a preserved railway. Today it could hardly fail.

7

A GNR Line across Staffordshire

Stafford/Chartley/Uttoxeter

In the early days of the Stafford & Uttoxeter Railway (S&UR) there were often difficulties over connections with London & North Western Railway (LNWR) trains at Stafford. To overcome this, the S&UR trains had to frequently increase speed when

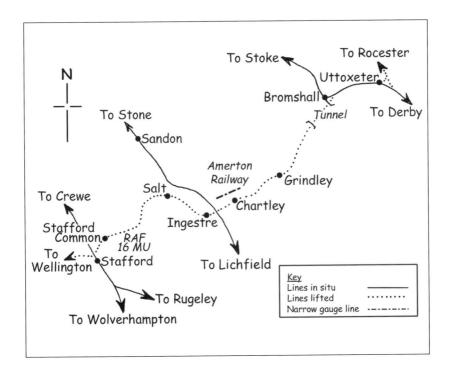

running late and it was such an instance that caused a bad accident in May 1868. A train was already behind time when leaving Uttoxeter and so the engine crew took Hopton Bank just prior to Stafford too fast. As a result the train was derailed on a curve at the end of the cutting.

Two crew members were killed, two were seriously injured and eight passengers were also hurt. In the book *The Stafford & Uttoxeter Railway*, P. Jones wrote that a report to the Board of Trade stated that the track might have been slightly 'out of gauge' due to heavy frost and the weight of the leading pair of locomotive's wheels was not enough to hold them down. The S&UR argued that since the LNWR refused to wait for connections, trains had to be driven hard especially if passengers travelling onward to Shrewsbury were aboard.

There was a further serious accident in March 1882 when a special train travelling from Derby was derailed at Chartley.

Chartley station in 1949. There was a serious accident in 1882 at Chartley when a train, travelling too fast, derailed. No passengers were seriously hurt but many horses in horse boxes were killed. (Stations UK)

Stirling locomotive 0-4-2 no 569 was hauling three coaches, 13 horse boxes and a brake van plus further horse boxes, these last being without proper vacuum brake control. Because of this the driver was advised to proceed with caution but, unaware that a passing loop had just been brought into use at Chartley, the driver entered the station too fast, causing a derailment.

All the horse boxes struck the platform, several horses were killed or injured and many vehicles broke up. No passengers were hurt, only shaken. Following the accident, it was recommended that all future passing loops should be built with facing points on the straight. Chartley's layout was altered accordingly and a 10 mph speed limit was introduced.

The Stafford and Uttoxeter Railway, known locally as the 'Clog and Knocker', was agreed by Parliament in July 1862. Construction was difficult, with the need for a tunnel near Bromshall (321 yds) and also a cutting at Hopton, where blasting

Salt station. Today the station has been completely demolished but the station-master's house has become a private residence. (Stations UK)

Ingestre station, on a former GNR line, c1948. Close by, the line crossed the NSR line from Rugeley to Stoke. (Stations UK)

through solid rock was necessary. The line opened on 23rd December 1867 and intermediate stations were built at Salt (known as Salt & Sandon after 1904), Ingestre, Stowe (renamed Chartley in 1874) and Grindley. Within the Act, a branch of almost two miles to Weston & Ingestre on the NSR had also been agreed and, subsequently, another to Abbot's Bromley to the south. Neither of these two additions was ever built.

Perhaps an explanation as to why the Stafford to Uttoxeter Railway was built at all was that the Great Northern Railway (GNR) hoped to provide a link between Central Wales and Uttoxeter and then on to the Nottinghamshire/Derbyshire coalfields. Such plans had been strongly opposed by the LNWR and the NSR, with the result that only a stretch between Stafford and Bromshall junction was ever completed. To reach Uttoxeter from Bromshall junction, trains had to run on NSR tracks.

Grindley station was on a Great Northern Railway (GNR) branch from Stafford to Uttoxeter. The station closed in December 1939, remaining open for freight until 1951. Today only a road bridge and embankments survive. (Stations UK)

In July 1874 a further station opened known as The Common (later known as Stafford Common) to cater for a growing population to the north of Stafford and also for passengers travelling to the nearby horse racing. Meantime the S&UR was running into financial difficulties and in 1879 a Bill allowed the GNR to use its tracks. This meant that, in addition, the GNR would use the section of NSR track from Bromshall junction to Uttoxeter; so in return it was agreed that the NSR could use S&UR lines. Traffic on the line increased but the S&UR had virtually lost its independence and, two years later in 1881, the GNR purchased the S&UR for £100,000.

With wider scope now possible, a service between Stafford and Derby commenced in November 1881 that connected with Nottingham, Grantham and Burton. The GNR took every opportunity to exploit its line, including the provision of many excursion trains to East Coast resorts. Early GNR locomotives

Former GNR Stafford Common station, 1949. The station was used by many passengers visiting the nearby horse racing. During the 1939/1945 war an RAF Unit was established in the area. (Stations UK)

seen on the line included 2-4-0s of class E2 built by Stirling at Doncaster in 1882, renowned for their 6 ft 7 in driving wheels. Soon after the turn of the century a Stirling class 0-6-0 was introduced.

Salt production had long been a feature in parts of Staffordshire, discovered in the Stafford Common area during water boring. It was not until around the turn of the century that a company established itself in this region to the south of the line, with further companies soon to follow. By 1913 over 81,000 tons of salt were being produced annually.

When war broke out in September 1939, the line was reduced to one train each way daily. On 4th December 1939 regular passenger services were completely withdrawn but the line acquired a new importance. An RAF unit was established not far from Stafford Common and, in addition, an army depot was set up at Bromshall, both with numerous sidings. The purpose of the RAF unit was to serve as a maintenance and supplies depot for RAF planes and equipment and a complex track layout was constructed.

The Air Ministry sidings remained busy after the war as overseas bases were wound down and equipment was returned for storage or disposal. At nationalisation in 1948, the line between Bromshall junction and the Air Ministry sidings closed, yet some nine years later, on 23rd March 1957, many enthusiasts were able to enjoy a 'last ride' on the branch. The Stephenson Locomotive Society (Midlands area) organised a three-coach push-pull set hauled by Ivatt 2-6-2T no 41224 to travel the line.

A journey along the former route reveals a few reminders of the past. At Stafford the bay that once housed Uttoxeter trains has become a car park. The station and trackbed at Salt have gone but the station-master's house has become a private residence. At Grindley, the road bridge and embankments can still be found. Uttoxeter is a pale shadow of its former self. Gone

A Stephenson Locomotive Society Special pauses at Bromshall West junction on 23rd March 1957, the last passenger train to cover the former Stafford to Uttoxeter line. (D.K. Jones Collection)

are the platform awnings, the footbridge, the sidings, the tall semaphore signals and the signal boxes. The line that swung northwards towards Rocester has also gone, with the former platform area partly replaced by a car park completed in the late 1980s. The two remaining platforms appear bare and uninviting, with their 'bus-stop' type shelters serving the few trains that ply daily between Stoke and Derby.

Although not strictly a 'lost' line, the Amerton Railway is worth a brief mention. It is located 6 miles north-east of Stafford, on the A518 Stafford–Uttoxeter road, approximately 1 mile from Weston, and is part of a 'working farm' visitor centre. The line is operated by the Staffordshire Narrow Gauge Railway Limited and it has a circular route of about one mile in length. Pride of

The locomotive 'Isabel' on the 2 ft gauge Amerton Railway to be found to the north-east of Stafford providing visitors with a one-mile round trip. (Photo courtesy Peter Bell)

place on the line is the locomotive *Isabel*, a product of W.G. Bagnall of Stafford, works no 1491 of 1897. Construction of the railway began in June 1990 and over the next two years volunteers built the 2 ft gauge railway on a greenfield site. Rolling stock includes numerous industrial locomotives, four toastrack coaches, a brake van and various wagons. The former Chartley station from the Stafford to Uttoxeter line has been erected following restoration to become a museum of Staffordshire narrow gauge railway history.

8

Lost Lines from Walsall and 'The Colliery Line'

Walsall/Cannock/Rugeley
Walsall/Brownhills/Lichfield/Wichnor junction
The Chasewater Railway

Walsall/Cannock/Rugeley

When trains reached Cannock from Walsall on 1st February 1858, Cannock was 'the end of the line'. Any travel across the Chase to the Trent Valley at Rugeley was laborious indeed, requiring a trek over rough roads. With coal being brought into production in the Hednesford area, this state of affairs did not last long for the coal had to be marketed and a link with the industrial Midlands was needed. Hundreds of navvies were soon at work, building embankments and cutting through gravel and soft sandstone to reach the London & North Western (LNWR) main line at Rugeley (Trent Valley). The Cannock/Rugeley line, which opened on 7th November 1859, was called the Cannock Mineral Railway and was worked by the LNWR. Ten years later, despite competition from the NSR, the LNWR took over the company.

The many mineral sidings feeding the Walsall–Rugeley line provided the route with much of its traffic. Trucks came to Hednesford from collieries such as West Cannock, Brereton or Cannock Wood, where they were marshalled into trains before starting out for destinations via Rugeley or Walsall. Miners were carried to and from the pits in what were known as 'paddy trains', which had wooden seats. These were necessary because in earlier times there were no pithead baths. The last of the trains

94

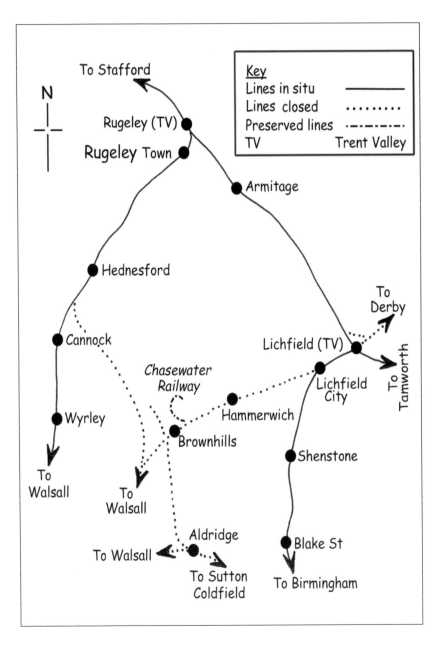

Walsall station on a wet day in March 1970. Northwards from Walsall, trains could leave for Lichfield or Rugeley. (John H. Meredith)

ran in the early 1920s with many men changing to buses, which ran directly to and from the pitheads.

Moors Gorse Halt between Hednesford and Rugeley became well known to many RAF servicemen during the Second World War when a camp was sited on nearby Brindley Heath. The lane from the halt leading up to the camp became affectionately known as 'Kitbag Hill'. After the war, traffic between Walsall and Rugeley dwindled but it was not until 18th January 1965 that the line closed to passenger traffic although freight traffic continued.

Almost a quarter of a century later, on 7th April 1989, the line re-opened from Walsall to Hednesford, recognising a need for commuter passenger traffic. Currently services have become available direct from Hednesford to Stafford. Diesel units carry passengers today – a far cry from the 'paddy trains' of yesteryear.

A deserted Cannock station in 1950, which closed in 1965. In earlier times the Rugeley to Walsall branch was much used by coal traffic. (Stations UK)

Locomotives pass at Hednesford station in steam days, c1952. The station survives today on the Walsall to Rugeley branch although the buildings have been demolished and rebuilt to a more basic structure. (Stations UK)

Walsall/Brownhills/Lichfield/Wichnor junction

The South Staffordshire Railway (SSR) opened a line from Walsall to Wichnor junction on 9th April 1849, where it joined the main Midland Railway route to Burton-upon-Trent, over which it had running powers. Intermediate stations opened at Rushall, Pelsall, Brownhills, Hammerwich and Lichfield. Later, in August, Lichfield Trent Valley station followed where the branch crossed the main line between Rugeley and Tamworth.

The line was in a way unique for, following disagreements within the SSR board, Parliament agreed the line could be leased to an individual, John McClean, for the unusually long period of 21 years. McClean was no newcomer to railways, having

Locomotive 45582 'United Provinces' leaves Lichfield Trent Valley on 23rd March 1957. (D.K.Jones Collection)

LNWR Hammerwich station, c1961, between Brownhills and Lichfield Trent Valley. The station closed in 1965. (Stations UK)

previously served as engineer to the broad gauge line constructed between Wolverhampton and Birmingham.

When McClean gave up his lease in 1861, ten years before expiry, the SSR transferred to the LNWR. This caused problems over the running rights previously enjoyed by the SSR from Wichnor junction to Burton-upon-Trent. The Midland Railway was not happy about the LNWR using its tracks and battles followed. Midland Railway men considered they treated their own engines with feeling and, as one Midland driver claimed, 'not like the rough and ready LNWR men who did dreadful things to their engines in the interests of speed, economy and punctuality'. The Midland Railway claimed comfort and cleanliness as priorities and considered that the trains the LNWR brought into Burton, often hauled by 'Cauliflower' 0-6-0 engines, were 'coal black and unkempt'.

The Midland Railway soon gave way and it is recorded that on the day in question an LNWR locomotive made 'a triumphal journal towards Burton'. Goods trains to Burton and later to

LNWR Shenstone station, c1910, on the line from Birmingham to Lichfield, originally built to serve Sir Richard Cooper at nearby Shenstone Court. During the First World War the Royal Train spent the night at Shenstone when King George V visited local troops. The building survives today, part of it in use as business premises. (John H. Meredith)

100

The former LNWR Brownhills station, c1950, between Walsall and Lichfield Trent Valley, which closed in 1965. Not far away was a Midland Railway Brownhills station, which closed in 1930. (Stations UK)

Derby soon became regular traffic and, in addition, an LNWR goods depot was established at Burton station. Yet rivalry between LNWR and Midland drivers continued for many years, even after 'grouping' in the 1920s. It is recorded that a former Midland driver, relaxing in his garden one summer evening, heard a locomotive with wheels slipping on a gradient and smoke billowing over him from what was previously an LNWR line. He was heard to comment, 'B——y North Western Man'!

The Walsall to Wichnor junction line closed to passenger traffic on 18th January 1965, the same day as the Walsall to Rugeley branch. A more up-to-date reminder perhaps came about with the reopening of the former line between Lichfield City and Lichfield Trent Valley in October 1989. This had made possible the use of BR's new class 323 four-coach units which provide a regular passenger service between Birmingham New Street and Lichfield Trent Valley, the latter connecting with the main Birmingham-avoiding Intercity line.

The Chasewater Railway

The Chasewater Railway operates passenger and demonstration freight trains in Chasewater Country Park, on the sole remaining section of the former Cannock Chase Coalfield mineral railway network. Although now regarded primarily as a vibrant visitor attraction, the Chasewater Railway plays an important role in recalling the importance of the coal mining industry in the area. Indeed, several of the railway's historic coaches were used to transport the local colliers to and from their place of work and, on appropriate occasions, the railway operates as 'The Colliery Line'.

The railway was originally founded in 1959, but was re-formed in 1985 as a registered charity. It is operated entirely by volunteers, some of whom have a personal association with the area's mining industry and the railway line in its 'original' form. Trains operate every Sunday and Bank Holiday Monday throughout the year, with industrial steam locomotives in regular use. Diesel trains operate during off-peak months and on summertime Saturdays.

The railway has successfully extended its running line in recent years, and now offers a round-trip journey of nearly four miles, between Brownhills West (the railway's headquarters) and Chasetown (Church Street). Further stations are provided at Norton Lakeside and Chasewater Heaths. Refreshments and shop facilities are available at both Brownhills West and Chasewater Heaths stations. A heritage centre and the railway's loco shed are also situated at Brownhills West. Despite its traditional appearance, the heritage centre is actually powered by solar energy, discreetly concealed in a mock water tank!

The railway is home to an interesting collection of industrial steam and diesel locomotives, including its two flagship steam locos, *Sentinel*, built in 1957, and *Asbestos*, a 1909-built 0-4-0ST. This locomotive recently received a full overhaul, enabling the railway to provide a frequent two-train service on steam gala dates. Several historic wooden-bodied carriages are housed in the heritage centre, including items dating back to 1875, while an

Chasewater Railway's steam locomotive 'Sentinel' takes on water at Brownhills West station. The Chasewater Railway in Chasewater Park near Walsall operates as a Colliery Line reflecting its origins and location in the heart of the Cannock Chase coalfield. (David Bathurst)

interesting range of freight wagons are also represented and used on demonstration trains.

In keeping with its colliery origins, the railway is in the process of constructing a narrow gauge line at Brownhills West, and has ambitions to provide a future railway link to the main car parks in the Country Park.

At the other extreme, the railway is providing facilities to enable Parry People Movers Ltd (PPM) of Cradley Heath to develop the company's Railcar no 12 and to assess passenger reaction to this innovative vehicle, which has been specifically designed for rural and branch line use. The company is seeking approval to operate Car 12 on the Stourbridge Town branch on a commercial basis.

A Parry People Mover being demonstrated at the Chasewater Railway. PPM vehicles are light tramway systems for smaller towns and can also be used on regional railways. (David Bathurst)

Chasewater Country Park itself has been upgraded significantly and, with the railway providing an interesting and enjoyable experience, a day visit is thoroughly recommended. Both the Country Park and the railway are signposted along the A5.

9

A Line from Shropshire

Wellington/Newport/Stafford

Locomotive no 45569 'Tasmania' hauls a passenger train at Stafford on Whit Monday 1953. The picture was taken before the station was rebuilt. (Russell Mulford)

There was a day in 1852 that villagers of Donnington, just to the north of Telford, would have long remembered. The trouble began at Shrewsbury when, on 29th July, a train from Stafford arrived with the driver complaining that the LNWR locomotive *Mazeppa* no 24, a 2-2-2 of Trevithic-Allan design built at Crewe in 1849, had problems. The foreman instructed the night cleaner,

106

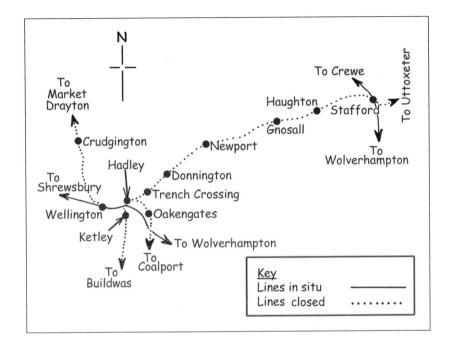

Thompson, to deal with it but early next morning, when the driver arrived to prepare the engine, he found it was missing. Thompson had earlier 'fired' *Mazeppa* but had left the engine in forward gear with the regulator open.

It was soon realised that the locomotive with no one aboard was steaming towards Stafford. There was an immediate hue and cry and another available engine was sent in hot pursuit. The driver saw flying steam in the distance but he could do nothing. It was not until Donnington that the runaway engine came to an unfortunate stop, crashing into the back of an early train bound for Stafford and killing one of the few passengers. Thompson was woken from his sleep at Shrewsbury to find himself facing a charge of manslaughter.

The line from Wellington to Stafford began its life by an Act of Parliament dated 3rd August 1846, submitted by the Shropshire Union Railways & Canal Company (SUR&CC). The company

Wellington station in the early 1950s. (Lens of Sutton)

Wellington's downside station building c1950, when trains could be caught directly to Stafford and beyond Market Drayton to Stoke. (Lens of Sutton)

was soon to become a pawn in the battles between the LNWR and the GWR to reach the Mersey. Less than a year later the SUR&CC was leased to the LNWR.

Earlier there had been numerous ambitious plans put forward by the SUR&CC, many of these comprising lines to be built along the banks of bankrupted canals. Such routes included a branch from Stafford to Stone in the Potteries, plus another between Crewe and Newtown in Wales. Canal owners had been forced to gradually give way to railway schemes as the railways proved themselves superior but the canal company's plans to convert further long stretches of canals never materialised.

The Wellington to Stafford line opened on 1st June 1849, the same day that services commenced between Shrewsbury and Oakengates. Most people welcomed the trains, which provided new links with the rest of the country, and it was expected that the agricultural and industrial trades would greatly benefit. The line from Stafford junction to Wellington was just over 18 miles in length and for a time it had the advantage that it was the only link between Shrewsbury and London. By taking a train to Stafford, passengers could continue on the LNWR to Euston. Three trains daily connected with London trains and this was doubled within a year or so. However, fares were not cheap. The second class cost to travel from Shrewsbury to Stafford was 3s 10d and the fare to London (also second class) was £1, a figure well above the average weekly wage. Third class or 'Parliamentary' trains were available but these generally left Shrewsbury between 3 am and 5 am in the morning, which to most was quite unacceptable.

Meantime the Shrewsbury & Birmingham Railway (S&BR) was struggling to reach Birmingham. Wet weather held up work on large embankments at Shifnal and also work in Oakengates tunnel. There was further aggravation when Sunday working was introduced, with clerics complaining it was a 'flagrant violation of the Sabbath'. It was to be another five years before Birmingham was reached but, when completed, it meant that passengers could travel 30 miles directly from Shrewsbury to Birmingham instead of 46 miles via Stafford. A bitter price war began and after massive reductions by the SUR&CC, the price

Trench Crossing station on the line from Wellington to Stafford. An LMS Fowler locomotive 2-6-4T hauls a passenger train in 1957. Trench Crossing station closed in September 1964. (Russell Mulford)

This is all that is left of Trench Crossing station in May 1992. The picture, taken looking towards Hadley, shows the remains of the platform for Stafford-bound trains. If planners succeed, this line could reopen at a future date to connect Wellington with an MOD depot at Donnington. (Russell Mulford)

dropped to as little as one penny for ten miles. People were quick to take advantage and trains into Shrewsbury from around Newport and Wellington were often carrying over a thousand passengers each!

The Wellington/Stafford line left the S&BR line at Stafford junction with its first intermediate station at Hadley. As a village, Hadley dates back to Saxon times and has numerous claims to fame. Hadley Park Mill, powered by both water and steam, was probably the only such mill of its kind in Shropshire and a lock at Hadley Park was last used in the 1930s. During the 18th century Hadley Park Hall was occupied by the celebrated ironmaster, John Wilkinson, who was well regarded by the local folk. So well, in fact, that many thought his ghost would return on the seventh anniversary of his death to pull the old industries out of a recession. Thousands gathered and waited (and still wait?) but he did not return.

After Trench Crossing and Donnington, the next station was Newport. Although a village, this was the only intermediate

LNWR Newport station, c1920, closed in September 1964. There is no sign of the station site today – only a nearby redundant road bridge survives east of the A41. (Stations UK)

111

In the 1950s scores of steam trains stopped at Wellington. Ex-LMS 2-6-2T hauls the 1.02 pm train from Crewe on 12th August 1963. (D.K. Jones Collection)

A train approaches Newport station in 1949. All that now remains of the station is a crane removed in 1973 to Blists Hill Open Air Museum at Ironbridge. (Stations UK)

station of any significance for, in later years, few passengers used the service beyond to Stafford. Today much of the former trackbed has gone and the station has been completely demolished to make way for a housing estate. Passing through Newport on the A41 it is possible to see a redundant road bridge to the east across a field. There is yet another reminder of Newport at the Blists Hill Museum at Iron Bridge. The station crane was removed there in 1973.

At Gnosall the embankments can be determined each side of the A518 on entering the village. The Shropshire Union Canal passes through Gnosall, linking Market Drayton and beyond to the north and Wolverhampton to the south. Gnosall's railway bridge across the A518 has gone but when in existence it carried the initials SUR (Shropshire Union Railways). Happily the station's down booking office has been saved, residing today in the main entrance to the Foxfield Railway at Caverswall Road station at Blythe Bridge in North Staffordshire. The last station before Stafford was Haughton. Although the area has

Haughton station in 1949 on the closed Wellington to Stafford line. Freight continued on the branch until August 1966 when the line was finally abandoned. (Stations UK)

Haughton station, looking towards Stafford. In early steam days nine trains stopped each way daily at Haughton travelling towards Stafford or Shrewsbury. (Stations UK)

considerably increased in population over the last few decades, it still retains much of its rural character. The manor house with its close-timbered black and white building dates back to the 16th century and the barn, now a cottage, boasts timbers reclaimed from sailing ships.

The Wellington/Stafford branch, like so many, fell victim to road competition and closed to passengers on 7th September 1964. Freight lingered awhile but this too closed between Newport and Stafford on 1st August 1966. Further stretches followed, leaving only the Wellington/Donnington section open. This was singled in July 1971 and track still exists today. During 2005 speculation existed that this section might be re-opened but much would need to be done.

10
A Line to Market Drayton

Stoke/Silverdale/Market Drayton

Earlier last century the village of Norton-in-Hales, close to the Shropshire/Staffordshire border, boasted three public houses and shops that included a butcher's, a general stores and a laundry. Not far away, where a lane climbed over a single-track railway line, could be found Norton-in-Hales station. Special trains used to run from Stoke bringing large crowds to the village for the annual harvest festivals and afterwards the

Norton-in-Hales station, on the North Staffordshire Railway, which closed in May 1956. (Late Tony Smith, Birch-Holland Collection, courtesy of Mark Smith)

Norton-in-Hales station, formerly on the Stoke/Market Drayton branch, is today a private residence. (Author)

Market Drayton Town Band played whilst a meal was provided under canvas in the rectory grounds.

Today the post office and all the shops have gone and there is only one pub, the Hinds Head. The railway has also long since gone. The station building plus part of the awning are still there, rescued by Dennis Parton and his wife, and the platform has become part of an attractive garden. But the railway spirit lives on for Dennis Parton, who has spent many years working for Network Rail, previously British Rail. Not far away can be found the former station-master's house.

When the North Staffordshire Railway (NSR) planned a freight line from Stoke to Silverdale, it was first necessary for the existing privately-owned Silverdale & Newcastle Railway (built in 1850 by ironmaster Ralph Sneyd without powers) to become public. Parliament agreed this by an Act of 1859, after which it was leased in March 1860 to the NSR and passenger services between Stoke and Silverdale commenced during 1862. It was initially intended to go no further, content to serve the various nearby collieries. But when the Great Western Railway (GWR) planned a line in 1862 from North Shropshire via Market Drayton to Manchester, the LNWR and NSR joined forces and blocked the idea. The GWR, not giving up easily, persisted but it was rejected by the House of Lords. As a result, the NSR felt it necessary to build westwards to Market Drayton to thwart any further GWR attempts. On 29th July 1864 Parliament agreed the NSR branch from Silverdale to Market Drayton.

On 1st February 1870 Market Drayton was reached from Stoke with an official opening for both goods and passenger traffic. This was not the first railway to reach Market Drayton, since GWR lines already existed from both Wellington and Nantwich,

NSR trains reached Market Drayton in 1870. But they were not the first to serve the town since trains came from Nantwich seven years earlier in 1863. (Lens of Sutton)

119

so celebrations were somewhat muted. In the book *The Stoke to Market Drayton Line*, C.R. Lester wrote of the various festivities that did take place. A commemorative public ball was held at the Corbet Arms assembly rooms in Market Drayton, and at Pipe Gate visitors from Silverdale were among the 30 guests who celebrated at the Chetwode Arms Inn with a dinner to mark the occasion. The toast was 'Success to the North Staffordshire Railway', and when the last train left Pipe Gate for Stoke at 8.35 pm few were on it. One may assume celebrations lasted well into the night with a number of bleary-eyed passengers on the 10.45 am the next morning.

Four trains ran each way on weekdays and two on Sundays with intermediate stations initially between Market Drayton and Silverdale at Norton-in-Hales, Pipe Gate (for Pipe Gate and Woore) and Keele (for Keele and Madeley). As well as providing a useful passenger service plus agricultural links, it was expected the line would further develop collieries plus bring North Staffordshire into direct communication with GWR lines. On the branch, the need for half-day excursions out of Stoke turned Norton-in-Hales into a health resort and it soon became popular with tourists looking for a country outing or as a place for 'Sunday School treats'.

Following the arrival of NSR trains, the original passenger station at Market Drayton was enlarged. It was rebuilt in a 'French Renaissance' style with ornamental ironwork and square-topped pavilions at each end. In later years through trains were operated via Market Drayton on GWR tracks to Hodnet on market days and often further south to places beyond Wellington. A 'small wayside station' opened later at Madeley. For a short time during 1871 the station was known as Madeley Manor, later to become Madeley Road for the rest of its life.

Pipe Gate became busy with trade in timber and cattle and in the 1880s a creamery and milk condensing plant was established. Services to Pipe Gate increased considerably when, in 1885, a racecourse was laid out on farmland about half a mile to the north of the station. Race trains came from many Midlands towns and extra staff were drafted in to cope with the crowds. Towards Stoke a small station called Keele Park was

Hodnet station which was served by GWR trains and also, on market days, by North Staffordshire Railway trains from Stoke. The nearby Hodnet Hall is well known for its lakeside gardens which attracted many visitors by train in earlier times. (Lens of Sutton)

Market Drayton station not long before closure. NSR services from Stoke closed in 1956 but GWR trains between Wellington and Nantwich, via Market Drayton, lasted until 1963. (Lens of Sutton)

121

NSR Silverdale station, which closed to passengers in March 1964 but remained open until the 1970s serving the adjacent colliery. (Stations UK)

Silverdale station, April 2005, photographed from a nearby footbridge. Only the platform edges can be determined. The station buildings and the adjacent goods sidings have all gone. (Author)

Silverdale colliery ceased working on 24th December 1998. Picture taken July 1998. (D.K. Jones Collection)

Madeley Road station, 1949, on the NSR Market Drayton branch from Stoke. The station, which closed to passengers in 1931, was not far from the former Madeley station on today's WCML. (Stations UK)

This was where Madeley Road station was sited. The area is occupied today by a railway engineers' building. The original Madeley Road station was known as Madeley Manor but this was changed to Madeley Road in 1871. (Author)

125

opened when Ralph Sneyd (son of the ironmaster – another Ralph) constructed a steeplechase course. Training and breeding stables were set up nearby and a horse loading dock was built at Keele Park station. The racecourse lasted until 1901 when Sneyd's family finances deteriorated.

Following the demands of the Silverdale and Apedale coal plants, a system of 'private' working was developed over NSR tracks. For many years a passenger service was provided for employees from Newcastle-under-Lyme to meet the various shifts and the train, usually ex-NSR four-wheeled coaches, became known as the 'Apedale Paddy'. There were numerous stops at places such as Brampton and Liverpool Road (opened 1905) plus other unofficial stops close to pits so that trains were often empty when reaching the Apedale terminus.

In 1905 a Beyer Peacock railcar was introduced to the Market Drayton branch as an economy measure. Many passengers had been lost owing to poverty in the area. Further halts were opened in an effort to attract passengers but, as the 1920s progressed, competition from road transport took its toll. The NSR (now LMS) provided additional trains but it was in vain. Early in 1956 British Rail announced closure of the line from Market Drayton to Silverdale and, despite efforts by a local Transport Users' Consultative Committee, the end for passenger traffic came on Saturday, 5th May.

As usual for a final day, the train carried its heaviest load for many years. As 2-6-4T locomotive no 42671 hauled four coaches from Market Drayton at 7 pm, the occasion was marked by exploding detonators. Along the line small groups of mourners watched the passing. Eighty-six years of service had come to an end although passenger services between the Silverdale and Stoke section lasted a further eight years until closure on 2nd March 1964.

Today a spur from the main Crewe to Stafford line survives, enabling freight trains to reverse at Madeley onto a section of the former Market Drayton branch to reach Silverdale. The spur includes three tunnels along its route, the longest being Keele tunnel of 684 yds. When the M6 was built in 1961 a single line bridge had to be built to carry the surviving track across the six motorway lanes just north of Keele. The station has gone from Keele but perhaps the name today implies more a motorway service area than a railway station – surely a sad reflection of our changing times.

11
A 'Switchback' Railway and a Tramway

The Burton and Ashby Light Railway
Burton Corporation Tramways

B&ALR car no 13, c1910, photographed at what is believed to be at the top of High Bank Road, Winshill, where it joins the Ashby Road. (Picture courtesy of the 'Burton Mail')

The Burton and Ashby Light Railway

Disaster struck at Burton-upon-Trent when a tram ran backwards down Winshill's Bearwood Hill Road to overturn dramatically in Newton Road. Two people died and 14 were injured as a result. The car was no 19 on the Burton & Ashby Light Railway system and the date was 8th October 1919.

The immediate outcome was the enforcement of a 4 mph speed limit whilst descending Bearwood Hill and the introduction of a compulsory stop halfway down the hill. Improvements were later made at the end of Burton Bridge so that the notorious double bend for the trams could be straightened out.

In addition large 'slipper' type magnetic brakes approximately 2 ft long were fitted to cars to replace the two small magnetic brake shoes used previously. Such was the efficiency of these that skidding was practically eliminated but they gave another problem. Burton also had a dense network of industrial railways to serve the many breweries and these included no fewer than eight level crossings. Apparently whilst crossing such a brewery track, there was an occasion when the magnets lifted a section completely out of the ground!

The Burton & Ashby Light Railway, introduced in 1906, came about despite many objections. Swadlincote complained it would interfere with their Saturday evening market and, earlier, the Midland Railway (MR) had complained it would compete with its parallel railway. When the line was authorised by Parliament on 5th November 1902, it was to be worked by the Midland Railway (subsequently the LMS) and it transpired that, instead of depleting Swadlincote's market, trams brought in considerable numbers of additional people.

Work to construct the line began in February 1905, at a total estimated cost of just under £90,000. Some 10 miles of track were built and the gauge was 3 ft 6 in. This was more out of necessity, since it was planned that trams would run through to Burton's town centre on the Corporation's tracks of 3 ft 6 in. As in Burton, overhead current collection was installed and, since several long stretches were included, colour signals were put in place, operated by trolley-wheel contact through a solenoid. The power station was at Swadlincote, next to the tram depot. Being in the centre of a colliery area, this ensured a good supply of cheap coal.

Services began on 13th June 1906 between Burton and Swadlincote and throughout from Burton to Ashby on 2nd July. The fare for the whole journey was 6d and a section of the journey was on reserved track across fields and a valley – hence the nickname 'The Sixpenny Switchback'. The fare was considerably less than the Midland Railway fare, which was unexpected since the trams were operated by the Midland in competition with its own trains. The line passed from Burton across fields to Newall and Swadlincote, continuing on through Woodville to a terminus outside Ashby-de-la-Zouche station. Later in 1906 a branch opened to Church Gresley, terminating at Gresley MR station. During the 10-mile journey, trams passed through three counties, Staffordshire, Derbyshire and Leicestershire.

The Burton & Ashby system commenced with 13 open-top cars, each built by Brush and seating 41 passengers and each

Reserved track passes through Swadlincote cutting, c1912, on the Burton & Ashby Light Railway. During its life the tramway inherited the name 'The Sixpenny Switchback'. (John H. Meredith)

130

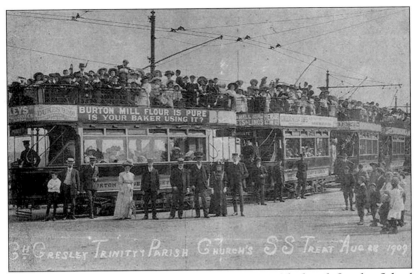

Trams are crowded for a Church Gresley Trinity parish church Sunday School treat, August 1909. (John H. Meredith)

powered by two Westinghouse 25 hp motors. In 1906 a further seven cars were bought, similar to the original ones, bringing the total fleet to 20. The trams were popular and from 1908 there were cars every ten minutes at peak periods. The maximum permitted speed was 12 mph but this was later increased to 18 mph along certain stretches. A local newspaper of the day stated, 'Much of the route is very picturesque and capital views can be got from cars when they are on the high portions of the line.'

By the early 1920s the tramway suffered, like many others, from bus competition. In addition the track was deteriorating badly from wear and it was clear the end could not be far off. Services were reduced, economies effected and fares were increased. The last car ran on 19th February 1927 and car bodies were for sale. Ten were sold to the Tynemouth & District Electric Traction Company although it is thought that only six were used.

B&ALR tramcar no 20 negotiates Market Street, Church Gresley. The car was built by Brush in 1906 and was powered by two 25 hp Westinghouse motors. (John H. Meredith)

Car no 13 photographed in Swadlincote, c1910. Trams first came to the Burton & Ashby Light Railway in June 1906. The fleet comprised 20 open-topped cars. (Picture courtesy of the 'Burton Mail')

Burton & Ashby Light Railway (B&ALR) track still survives on the drive to the former Ashby railway station. (Author)

Burton Corporation Tramways

Burton Corporation commenced its own tramway system in 1903. Tracklaying began in the town in September 1902, during which time traffic became very congested. After the lines had been laid in their concrete foundations, Station Street and the High Street were paved with wooden blocks. This work led to more problems with many complaints about noise. When completed the system comprised nearly seven miles of track with a gauge of 3 ft 6 in.

Services commenced on 3rd August 1903 when the Mayoress, Mrs Morris, drove the first car. A newspaper reported, 'The motor commenced throbbing and to mighty cheers from the dense throng of people, the first tram moved gracefully towards

A tramcar crosses Burton Bridge over the river Trent (not The Trent Bridge as wrongly identified). B&ALR trams, 3 ft 6 in gauge, ceased running in February 1927. (Picture courtesy of the 'Burton Mail')

Former track from the Burton tramway found in Bearwood Hill Road during recent road works. This section was used by B&ALR trams, as well as Burton Corporation Tramways. (Nigel Oppitz)

the centre of the town.' Initially the fleet comprised 20 open-top cars, each fitted with two 25 hp motors. All were four-wheel double-deck, with seating for 43 passengers. Services were along Station Street, one then going northwards to Horninglow, another southwards along Branston Road. Two further routes crossed the river to Stapenhill and Winshill. A further service later climbed High Bank Road from the Winshill branch terminus to link with the Burton & Ashby Light Railway in Ashby Road.

The fare from Station Street to Stapenhill was 1d, and 1½d to travel on to the terminus in Wellington Street. A motorman's typical wage in 1903 was 5½d an hour so a driver could earn nearly £2 for an 86-hour week. It has to be recalled, however, that these were days when beer would cost 3d a pint!

Two decorated Burton Corporation trams, believed to be celebrating King George V's Coronation. (Picture courtesy of the 'Burton Mail')

In 1920 a further four cars were ordered, each fitted with two 30 hp motors. These were 46-seaters and equipped with balconies. Top deck covers were gradually added to most of the fleet but those on the Winshill route remained open-top throughout.

The Corporation's tramway system lasted only 26 years, by which time the trams had been replaced by buses. The last tram ran down from Winshill on New Year's Eve 1929, after which car bodies were lined up in New Street car park and labelled 'For Sale, Cheap'. The bodies were recommended for use as sports pavilions or garden shelters but four of them found a better use. The last four cars purchased in 1920 were sold to York Corporation where they ran until 1934.

A surviving tram column carrying the Midland Railway crest which can be found today at Sunnyside in Newhall. (Author)

Much evidence remains of the two Burton systems. The entrance to Burton Corporation's tram depot is the new extension to the Justice of the Court in Horninglow Street. The depot itself is used to house police vehicles but the tracks, pits and pulleys are still there, unfortunately not available for inspection. On the Burton & Ashby system, a trolley pole carrying the Midland Railway crest still stands at Sunnyside in Newhall and at Ashby station drive, track survives leading appropriately into the front garden of a house called 'Tramways'.

12
Lost Lines from Burton

Burton-upon-Trent/Tutbury
Burton-upon-Trent/Swannington/Leicester

A passenger train awaits departure at Burton-upon-Trent station, c1910. Burton was an important main line station, as well as serving branches to Tutbury and Leicester. (Stations UK)

Burton-upon-Trent/Tutbury

There was a time when Burton-upon-Trent's most important rail traffic was its beer. The brewery trade took full advantage of the railway system with most of the town's breweries linked to the main line by a complex system of branches and sidings. The lines, worked by saddle tank locomotives, brought congestion to

139

An almost deserted platform 4 at Burton-upon-Trent, 1955. Apart from passenger services, Burton boasted many goods yards, sidings and sheds. (Stations UK)

road traffic due to the large number of level crossings. The breweries were requiring over a thousand wagons a day.

Brewing began in local monasteries and by the 17th century Burton beer was being drunk in London. During the 18th century Burton's beer became known in many countries abroad – the furthest afield being Russia. The well-known Bass Brewery opened in Burton in 1777 producing 2,000 barrels a year. The railway became a vital part in the marketing of beer and from the 1860s most breweries had sidings. By 1900 freight traffic from Burton consisted of many trains carrying beer barrels to many parts of the country, including three fast services daily to London. During the October brewing period, casks were stored in vaults built for the purpose under St Pancras station.

Over the years freight services from Burton increased considerably. As well as beer, traffic included timber, plaster slabs, engineering and chemical products but as road traffic

Locomotive 43763 hauls a freight train past Burton-upon-Trent station, June 1958. Burton remains a prominent brewery town; in the background the Ind Coope & Allsop factory can be seen. (D.K. Jones Collection)

gradually took over the services were cut back. Also earlier last century passenger services were being drastically reduced. A further hazard to the Burton railway systems was when the NSR locomotive shed was badly bombed in 1916. The main line has, however, remained an important link between the East Midlands, the Potteries and the North-West.

During the 1920s around 150 main line passenger trains either left or called at Burton station each day. The town's original station was completed in 1839 following the opening of the Birmingham & Derby Junction Railway. The station was rebuilt in 1883 at the same time as Station Bridge, which crosses over the tracks. Burton station became well known as a place where lunch or tea baskets could be ordered in advance and taken to the train by attendants. For 3/3d a basket comprised a chop or steak with vegetables, cheese, butter, fruit etc, plus a bottle of

Horninglow station on the Burton to Tutbury branch, photographed 1949. After closure the station building became a café. (Stations UK)

beer or wine. When so-called modernisation came in 1971 Burton station lost its buildings, canopy and its fine wrought-iron work.

The 5½ mile branch line to Tutbury was one of Burton's least important passenger services yet it is still remembered by many today. Visit Horninglow, a few miles out of Burton, and the Jennie Inn can be found close to where trains once stopped at an intermediate station on their journey to Tutbury. The line no longer exists and the pub is one of the few reminders. The passenger service began on 11th September 1848 and lasted well over a century. In its earliest days the line was run by the North Staffordshire Railway (NSR) and after 'grouping' by the London, Midland & Scottish Railway (LMS).

The 'Tutbury Jennie' usually comprised a small tank locomotive and one, two or three non-corridor coaches. Later 'push-pull' motor trains were introduced, avoiding the need for the engine to change ends. Intermediate stations were at Horninglow, Stretton & Clay Mills and Rolleston-on-Dove but all

Rolleston-on-Dove. On 1st January 1949 all the intermediate stations on the Tutbury branch closed. Passenger services on the branch were withdrawn on 13th June 1960. (Stations UK)

Stretton & Clay Mills station on a cold day, 1900. After closure of the branch in 1960 the trackbed was converted into a road, completed 1983. (Stations UK)

these closed on 1st January 1949. The service carried on until 11th June 1960 when local people turned out in force to bid farewell to a much loved line. The locomotive was a 1950 Crewe-built 2-6-2T no 41277 and on its last run back to Burton there were some 500 people in the three coaches. To add to the merriment one passenger blew a bugle during the whole journey.

Burton-upon-Trent/ Swannington/Leicester

There was an embarrassing happening on 17th July 1832 when the first section of the Leicester and Swannington Railway ceremonially opened between Leicester (West Bridge station) and Bagworth. A small brass cannon was fired as the first train left, with the directors sitting on boardroom chairs placed in a wagon. Others sat on planks and some stood. The band played and other onlookers waved banners bearing slogans saying 'Cheap coal and granite', 'Warm hearths and good roads' and 'May the triumph of the science prove the blessing of people'. According to local reports, when the locomotive reached a tunnel at Glenfield its chimney hit the low roof. Robin Leleux wrote in his book *A Regional History of the Railways of Great Britain: The East Midlands*: 'The band stopped playing, the light bonnets, veils and dresses of the ladies, and shirt fronts and faces of the men were covered in smuts.' The train made an unscheduled stop by a brook while the company washed, using handkerchiefs as towels. After that, events ran more smoothly. There were refreshments at Bagworth – cold meat for the men but cakes and wine for the ladies. On the return to Leicester dinner was available for fifty gentlemen.

The 16-mile Leicester and Swannington Railway was authorised in May 1830. It came about because the Leicestershire miners were not happy with coal from Derbyshire being imported into the town of Leicester instead of their own. The Leicestershire miners tried to overcome the problem by opening two tramways and the Charnwood Forest Canal but the canal

144

burst its bank in 1799 and was never repaired. Yet canal owners persisted with ideas to market their coal locally and, after a visit by canal owner William Stenson of Whitwick to the Stockton and Darlington Railway, plus a meeting with George Stephenson, a solution was found and the Leicester and Swannington Railway came about.

Although the line from Leicester initially ran from the west bank of the river Soar near West Bridge to Bagworth, the route was soon extended to Long Lane (Coalville), opening on 22nd April 1833 for goods and five days later for passengers. The route included inclines at Bagworth and Swannington and the short tunnel at Bagworth. Passengers were not encouraged and coal transport was considered the line's primary objective. Partly because of this there was a further unfortunate incident in 1833. A local newspaper reported that on 5th August 1833 a large party hired a carriage to take them to Bardon Hill. On their return they found it full and the party had to climb on the coal wagons to travel back to Leicester. It was raining quite hard and

Leicester West Bridge station was the terminus of the Burton–Leicester branch. It was not a significant station, sited away from the Leicester Midland main line and across the river. (Stations UK)

145

the ladies in their silks and white dresses 'cut a laughable figure'. The newspaper said it was time that such complaints were brought to the attention of the directors.

The line was bought in 1846 by the Midland Railway, which saw it as a means to provide a direct link between Leicester and Burton-upon-Trent. The company considered such a move necessary to counter lines being planned by the rival LNWR linking the coal mining areas with Nuneaton to the south and Loughborough to the north. But there were still obstacles for the Midland Railway. It became necessary to build bypass lines to avoid the Bagworth incline and the low-roofed tunnel at Glenfield. A year later a line from Desford to Leicester via Kirby Muxloe was opened. This section not only bypassed Glenfield tunnel but it enabled trains to join the existing Leicester to Rugby line south of the city rather than extend the old line from West Bridge. The benefit to the miners as well as to commerce in Leicester was felt immediately. Derbyshire coal had sold at 18s a ton whereas Leicestershire coal now sold at 11s a ton. The Leicester to Burton line opened throughout on 1st August 1849.

Desford, 1949. Although the station closed completely in 1964, Desford to Blackpool excursions continued to cover the line for some years. (Stations UK)

Moira station, 1961. The Burton–Leicester branch had many steep gradients, tight curves, cuttings and two tunnels. In the early 1920s a 4-mile journey from Moira to Swadlincote took almost 20 minutes. (Stations UK)

The remains of Swannington station in 1972 on the former Burton to Leicester branch. A section of the track on the branch can be seen today at the Science Museum in London. (Stations UK)

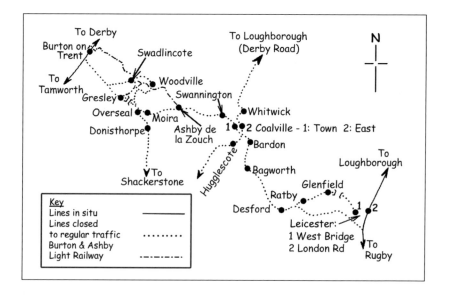

A loop line to serve goods traffic in the Swadlincote area opened in 1880 and this served passengers from 1883. This line was extended to form a complete loop with stations at Swadlincote and Woodville in 1884. Construction was difficult, involving steep gradients, tight curves, cuttings and two tunnels. Locomotives were generally 0-6-0T or LMS 2-6-4 tank engines. Passenger traffic soon dwindled, with nothing but just meandering between brick kilns and slag heaps to look out on. In the early 1920s a 4-mile journey from Moira to Swadlincote took almost 20 minutes. The loop line closed to regular passenger traffic in 1947 although Desford to Blackpool excursions continued to cover the line for some years. Passenger and goods traffic ended in March 1964 when the line closed completely although part of the western section remained in use for access to Cadley colliery.

In the 1920s a train could be caught at Burton to arrive at Leicester after 1¼ hours, stopping at all intermediate stations. Many years later there had been hopes that the Burton to Leicester line might reopen to passenger traffic. Currently it is infrequently used by heavy freight traffic. Plans announced in the 1990s included an hourly service of Sprinter trains stopping at the 16 new stations planned along the route. It is reckoned that such a service could carry up to 1.8 million passengers a year. It would be known as the Ivanhoe Line or the National Forest Line. The Ivanhoe Line would adopt its name from Sir Walter Scott's famous novel centred on the castle at Ashby de la Zouche. Thus Ivanhoe, the novel's hero, could become the emblem for what is considered would be the biggest local rail service development project seen anywhere in the country (apart from the largest cities) since the railways were first built.

However, current progress does not look encouraging. Leicester County Council says that while in the longer term it proposes to reintroduce passenger trains on the Leicester to Burton 'Ivanhoe' Line, this could only come about 'should conditions change to make the scheme affordable'. The Council states that rail industry costs have increased somewhat since the proposals in the late 1990s and the current national rail policy focus is on key inter-urban routes, mainly involving London.

Conclusion

The decline of many branch lines began in the 1920s. Buses were able to offer a more flexible service than the trains and road haulage was on the increase. In addition, the private motor car was beginning to make its presence felt. After nationalisation in 1948, the railways, still recovering from the demands of war service, were slow to meet any competition and were losing ground. Reduced revenue was leading to increased economies and then closures, with the entire pattern of inland transport gradually changing.

In March 1963 proposals were made in a report that became popularly known as the 'Beeching Plan'. Basically the idea was to keep lines considered suitable to rail traffic and give up the remainder. It was claimed that one third of the rail system in Britain carried only 1% of the total traffic! Further drastic cuts inevitably followed and many more branch lines disappeared. Closures – at first a trickle – became a torrent. Where branches once existed, some linking major routes across the region, soon only the original trunk routes remained. A few branch lines have survived but their future must surely be considered as uncertain.

What are the possibilities for the future in the area? Thought has been given to plans for the reintroduction of passenger services between Loughborough, Leicester, Burton-upon-Trent and Derby. To be known as the Ivanhoe Line, an hourly service of Sprinter trains has been considered, with numerous new stations proposed. Costs were estimated at up to £15 million and it was anticipated that up to nearly 2 million passengers could be carried annually. Leicester County Council had ideas to have a service operational in stages in 1994 and 1995 but as is known this did not come about. In 2005 the Council cited increased rail industry costs as the reason.

Passenger traffic recommenced between Walsall, Cannock and Hednesford in April 1989 and between Lichfield City and Lichfield Trent Valley in October 1989. Services were extended from Hednesford to Rugeley in 1997 and then northwards to Stafford in October 1999. Although just out of Staffordshire there is encouraging news concerning the former Wellington to Stafford line. The Department of Transport has given the go-ahead to a Telford Railfreight project. The scheme will reinstate the railway from Wellington to Donnington and create a modern freight interchange facility on land part-owned by the Ministry of Defence. The terminal will divert around half a million tonnes of freight a year to rail.

Any moves to get freight or, indeed, passenger traffic off the roads and back to rail must surely be encouraged. Successive governments have taken little interest in our rail system to the point that the railways have become run down. To the author, who has just researched Staffordshire and suffered very heavy traffic, frequent hold-ups, lorries of ever-increasing size and weight plus the added burden of continual speed traps, any move back to the railways can only be good news.

It is almost 150 years since railways came to Staffordshire. What a downhill path many lines have taken since the days of the Great Western or the London, Midland & Scottish Railways – or, even earlier, since the proud days of the 'Knotty'.

Opening and Final Closure Dates of Lines to Regular Passenger Traffic

Line	Opened	Final Closure	
Burton-upon-Trent/Tutbury	11 Sep 1848	13 June 1960	
Walsall/Brownhills/Lichfield/ Wichnor jct	9 Apr 1849	18 Jan 1965	*1
Wellington/Newport/Stafford	1 June 1849	7 Sep 1964	
Uttoxeter/Leek/North Rode	13 Jul 1849	4 Jan 1965	
Burton-upon-Trent to Leicester	1 Aug 1849	Mar 1964	
Rocester/Ashbourne	31 May 1852	1 Nov 1954	*2
Walsall/Cannock	1 Feb 1858	18 Jan 1965	*3
Cannock/Hednesford/Rugeley	7 Nov 1859	18 Jan 1965	*3
Market Drayton/Nantwich	20 Oct 1863	9 Sep 1963	
Stoke/Bucknall/Congleton	1 Jun 1864	11 Jul 1927	
Wellington/Market Drayton	16 Oct 1867	9 Sep 1963	
Bucknall/Endon/Leek	1 Nov 1867	7 May 1956	
Stafford/Chartley/Uttoxeter	23 Dec 1867	4 Dec 1939	
Silverdale/Market Drayton	1 Feb 1870	5 May 1956	
Stoke/Silverdale	7 Apr 1862	2 Mar 1964	

Etruria/Tunstall/Kidsgrove	15 Nov 1875	2 Mar 1964
Silverdale/Audley/Harecastle	28 Jun 1880	27 Apr 1931
Harecastle/Sandbach	3 Jul 1893	28 Jul 1930
Ashbourne/Parsley Hay	1 Jun 1894	1 Nov 1954
Cresswell/Cheadle	1 Jan 1901	17 Jun 1963
Waterhouses/Hulme End	27 Jun 1904	12 Mar 1934
Leek/Waterhouses	1 Jul 1905	30 Sep 1935
Burton-upon-Trent/Ashby	2 Jul 1906	19 Feb 1927 *4
Trentham/Trentham Park	1 Apr 1910	11 Sep 1939

*1 Lichfield City to Lichfield Trent Valley re-opened to passenger traffic October 1989.

*2 Emergency winter services continued between Rocester and Ashbourne for a number of years after official closure.

*3 Line connecting Walsall, Cannock and Hednesford re-opened to passenger traffic, April 1989. Services were extended from Hednesford to Rugeley in 1997.

*4 Burton & Ashby Light Railway.

Bibliography

In compiling *Lost Railways of Staffordshire*, I have referred to numerous sources, many now out of print, which include the following and which can be recommended for further reading:

Anderson, P. Howard *Forgotten Railways: The East Midlands* (David & Charles)

Baker, Allan C. *The Potteries Loop Line* (Trent Valley Publications)

Baker, Allan C. *The Cheadle Railway* (The Oakwood Press)

Christiansen, Rex *Forgotten Railways: The West Midlands* (David & Charles)

Christiansen, Rex *A Regional History of the Railways of Great Britain, Vol 7: The West Midlands* (David & Charles)

Jenkins, S.C. *The Leek & Manifold Light Railway* (The Oakwood Press)

Jeuda, Basil *The Leek, Caldon & Waterhouses Railway* (The North Staffordshire Railway Company)

Jones, P. *The Stafford & Uttoxeter Railway* (The Oakwood Press)

Keys, R. and the NSR Society *The Churnet Valley Railway* (Moorland Publishing Co)

Leleux, Robin *A Regional History of the Railways of Great Britain, Vol 9: The East Midlands* (David & Charles)

Lester, C.R. *The Stoke to Market Drayton Line* (The Oakwood Press)

INDEX

Moors Gorse Halt 96

New Haden colliery 45, 46, 48
Newport station 111, 114
Norbury & Ellaston station 66
North Staffordshire Railway 11, 12, 16, 25, 29, 31, 33, 34, 38, 39, 42, 45, 46, 49, 56, 57, 64, 66, 75, 79, 81, 88, 89, 94, 118, 119,126, 141, 142
North Staffordshire Railway Company (1978) Ltd 11, 28, 36, 71
Norton Bridge station 12, 16
Norton-in-Hales 117, *118*, 120
NSR: see North Staffordshire Railway

Oakamoor 36, 62

'paddy' trains 94
Park Hall 34
'parliamentary' trains 109
Parry People Movers Ltd 104
    railcar *105*
Parton, Dennis 118
Penkridge viaduct 15
Pinnox branch line 33, 35
Potteries, the 11, 16, 33
    loop line 28, 33, **37–40**, 44, 45

Pullman cars 11, *53*

Radway Green 29, 31
Rastrick, John 14
Rocester 62–63
    – Parsley Hay 64–66
Rolleston-on-Dove station 142, *143*, 144
Royal Scot, The 16
Rudyard Lake Railway 63–64, 82;
    stations 58
Rugeley 14, 94, 96, 98
Rushton station 58

Salt (& Sandon) station *87*, 88, 91
Sandbach 22, *25*, 27, 28
Sentinel 103, *104*
'sharp tanks' 39
Shenstone station *100*
Shrewsbury 109
    & Birmingham Railway 109, 111
    Earl of 62
Shropshire Union Canal 114
    Shropshire Union Railways & Canal Co 107, 109
Silverdale 22, 72, *122–124*
    & Newcastle Railway 118
    colliery 24, *124*
'Sixpenny Switchback' 130
Sneyd, Ralph, ironmaster 118, 119;
    jnr 126